THE ANTI-BOREDOM CHRISTMAS BOOK

Andy Seed

Illustrated by
Scott Garrett

Sky Pony Press
New York

To the children and staff of
St Wilfrid's RC Primary School, York

Copyright © 2016 Bloomsbury Publishing Plc
Text © 2016 Andy Seed
Illustrations © 2016 Scott Garrett
Additional illustrations © Shutterstock
First Sky Pony Press Edition Copyright © 2019

Sky Pony Press books may be purchased in bulk at special discounts for sales promotion, corporate gifts, fund-raising, or educational purposes. Special editions can also be created to specifications. For details, contact the Special Sales Department, Sky Pony Press, 307 West 36th Street, 11th Floor, New York, NY 10018 or info@skyhorsepublishing.com.

Sky Pony® is a registered trademark of Skyhorse Publishing, Inc.®, a Delaware corporation.

Visit our website at www.skyponypress.com.

10 9 8 7 6 5 4 3 2

Library of Congress Cataloging-in-Publication Data is available on file.

Cover design by Scott Garrett

ISBN: 978-1-5107-5470-6
Ebook ISBN: 978-1-5107-5473-7

Printed in the United States of America

IMPORTANT:
The author and publisher recommend enabling SafeSearch when using the Internet in conjunction with this book. We can accept no responsibility for information published on the Internet.

NOTE
Make sure you always ask an adult before using scissors.

CONTENTS

INTRODUCTION

Christmas is a time of giving, unwrapping, celebrating, eating, singing, and enjoying fun movies you've already seen six times. But it's also a time of waiting, traveling, and watching far too much TV. So why not switch off the box, dive into this book, and start having fun.

Inside you'll find LOADS of brilliant stuff to do including games, challenges, quizzes, and creative ideas. There are also jokes, amazing facts, and things to guess and score, all connected with Christmas (unsurprisingly). This is an ideal book to share with friends or to take with you on that long, dull journey to see Aunt Periwinkle and Uncle Buster.

For most of the activities you don't need anything at all—just a person or two. But if you want to, you can turn to the back of the book where you will find plenty of space to scribble, doodle, and write. This Christmas turn the fun-ometer up to the MAX!

LET IT SNOW

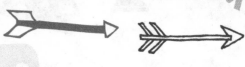

Score

How do you rate these wintery things?

Brr!

Give each of the below a score out of ten:

Snow   Ice

   The North Wind

Frost   Hail

  Making snowmen

Skiing   Sledging

Star ratings

Winter time means lots of layers! Give the coats below a star rating:

❄	I'd rather freeze
❄ ❄	Not me at all
❄ ❄ ❄	I suppose I could wear it
❄ ❄ ❄ ❄	My kind of coat
❄ ❄ ❄ ❄ ❄	Gimme gimme gimme!

Bomber jacket   Padded jacket

   Rain jacket   Parka

Waxed jacket   Ski suit

  Fleece   Waterproof onesie

    Duffle coat   Quilted jacket

Talk

How do your winter favorites compare with other people's?

Season reasons
- What's your favorite season and why?
- What's the best thing about winter?
- What's the worst thing about winter?

Weather you like it...
- If you could change the weather what would you do?
- What's your best memory of snow?
- What would you do if the weather was icy all the time?

Beating the cold
- What mega-warm clothing would you love to have?
- Do you like a real fire or central heating best?
- Can you come up with an invention to beat the winter chills?

Guess

See who's best at guessing these facts and figures about extreme winter weather—the nearest wins.

1. January 2010 was one of the coldest months in Britain ever. Can you guess how many centimetres of snow fell on the 6th January in the worst affected parts of southern England?
(40 centimeters)

2. The deepest snow ever recorded was in the mountains of California in 1911. Guess how deep it was in meters.
(11.5 meters)

3. The deepest snow recorded in Britain was in 1947. Guess how deep it was in meters.
(2.1 meters)

4. Guess how many centimetres wide the largest hailstone ever recorded was?
(20.5 centimeters)

5. In 1963 the sea froze along part of the English Channel coast. How far out to sea did it freeze at its maximum?
(5.4 miles)

Choose

It's time to pick your favorite from each pair below.
Get your friends and family to pick too!

Winter holidays
Would you rather go to:
⊙ The North Pole or Antarctica?
⊙ See penguins or polar bears?
⊙ Finland or Greenland?
⊙ The Alps or The Rockies?
⊙ The Ice Hotel (it's made of ice!)
or The Winter Olympics?

Winter gear
Would you rather have:
⊙ A plastic sledge or a wooden sledge?
⊙ Skis or a snowboard?
⊙ Ice skates or an ice hockey stick?
⊙ A snowmobile or a dog sled team?
⊙ A go at bobsleigh or curling?

Winter pottiness
Would you rather:
⊙ Eat an icicle or a giant hailstone?
⊙ Have a yeti for a pet
or a mammoth?
⊙ Wear frozen undies
or sleep in a bed of snow?
⊙ Wash in an ice bath
or a sleet shower?
⊙ Be a penguin or a walrus?

Challenges

Making a snowman

If there's plenty of snow on the ground you can follow this recipe to create a classic snowman.

1 To make the body, start by making a big snowball. It will need to be about as big as a football.

2 Now carefully roll your giant snowball in the snow, turning it in different directions as you go to gather as much snow as possible.

3 Keep doing this until you have a huge heavy snowball too big to push anymore. Pile some more snow on top of this to make it taller.

4 Roll another smaller snowball for the head. Place this on top of the giant snowball and pack snow in tight to make a neck so it won't roll off.

5 Now add details to make it look like a person:

✱ Two eyes (use two big stones or some coal)
✱ A nose (traditionally a carrot)
✱ A mouth (a row of small stones)
✱ A hat and scarf (always ask permission first before using these!)
✱ Buttons (more sticks or stones)
✱ Some people even use branches for arms

Silly faces
Instead of the usual things, can you think up the silliest things you could use to make a snowman's face?

Get creative

Give this snowman a stylish new look. It can be as wacky and weird as you like!

Lists

Here's how to say 'snow' in eighteen different languages. Challenge your friends and family to see how many they know!

Danish	sne
Dutch	sneeuw
Estonian	lumi
French	neige
German	Schnee
Hungarian	hó
Icelandic	snjór
Italian	neve
Irish	sneachta
Latin	nix
Maori	hukarere
Romanian	zăpadă
Slovenian	sneg
Spanish	nieve
Swedish	snö
Turkish	kar
Welsh	eira
Zulu	iqhwa

Amazing facts

White Christmases

In the UK snow is more likely in March than December.

People now bet on whether a snowflake will fall on Christmas Day in different locations around the UK, for example Buckingham Palace in London or Coronation Street in Manchester.

Amazingly, if half a meter of snow falls on Christmas Eve and stays on the ground over December 25th, this does not count as a white Christmas according to the Met Office (the UK's official weather organization) unless snow actually falls on Christmas Day too!

The last White Christmas in the UK was in 2010 when snow covered about 80 percent of the country.

The song White Christmas (sung by legendary crooner Bing Crosby) is the biggest selling single of all time.

Quiz

How much of a winter fan are you? Find out right here:

1. You look out of the window and it's snowing. Do you:
a) Wail
b) Say 'Yippee!'
c) Start polishing the sledge

2. You're at the top of a snowy mountain wearing skis. Do you:
a) Call 911
b) Walk down to the gentler slopes
c) Hurl yourself off, shouting 'Outamyway!'

3. Next door have built a giant snowman. Do you:
a) Ignore it and watch TV
b) Go round and admire it
c) Hire a digger and build a life-size snow T-Rex

4. The pond in your garden has frozen. Do you:
a) Yawn
b) Crack the ice to help the fish
c) Go curling

5. Your granny moves to the North Pole. Do you:
a) Laugh
b) Buy her some extra tights
c) Move in right away

6. The weather presenter announces a new ice age is on the way. Do you:
b) Make plans to live on Venus
c) Put on a woolly hat
d) Partay!

What your answers mean:
Mostly 'A's
You're not really a winter fan at all, are you?
Mostly 'B's
Let's give you a badge that says 'Sensible'.
Mostly 'C's
Tell us the truth: you're an Eskimo, aren't you?

15

Lists

Sensible and silly winter sports

Can you add any more to this list?

Sensible sport	Silly sport
Ice dancing	Mice dancing
Figure skating	Bigger skating
Snowboarding	Snowbearding
Ice hockey	Ice choccy
Bobsleigh	Gobsleigh
Curling	Uncurling
Ski jump	Ski trump

Jokes

What do snowmen eat
for dinner?
Icebergers

Why is snow clumsy?
It's always falling

What do snowmen wear on
their heads?
Ice caps

Where do Eskimos like
to shop?
Iceland

What's a
polar bear's
favorite shape?
An Arctic circle

What's a snowman's
favorite breakfast?
Frosties

How does an Eskimo fix
his broken home?
Igloos it

What would you call a
snowman on holiday in
Spain?
A puddle

Challenges

Build an igloo

Igloos are much harder to make than snowmen! You'll need about four people to help and a lot of snow! Melting snow works best for this. Ask an adult to help you with this activity as it can be a bit tricky.

1 Roll a series of snowballs in the same way as you start a snowman (see page 10). These should be about the size of basketballs.

2 Place the snowballs together in a circle about two meters across, leaving a gap for the entrance.

3 Using handfuls of extra snow, fill in the gaps between the snowballs and pack it in tight so that you have a smooth outer surface.

4 The top of this first layer of snowballs needs to be flat so that the flat surface leans inwards at a slight angle. You can do this by scraping it with a hard flat object such as a piece of wood, a ruler or a trowel (don't use your hand and always ask permission before doing this).

5 Place another layer of snowballs on top of the first layer, following this pattern:

* These snowballs should be a little smaller (football size).
* They should be placed slightly inward from the first layer so that the circle they make is smaller.
* The gaps between them need to be filled in as before.
* Smooth the top at an angle again.

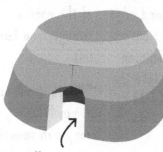

6 Continue in this way, adding layers, each smaller than the last, each leaning in as much as possible. It is very important to fill in all the gaps (inside and out) using wet sticky snow, pressed in hard.

7 Make a small circular entrance (don't try to build a small tunnel).

8 Once you are up to shoulder height the igloo roof should be leaning right in. The final block will need to be supported from underneath—ask an adult to help with this part.

Now you should have a fully-formed igloo! Make sure to take lots of photos before it melts!

Get Creative

How to make paper snowflakes

What's clever about this is that every paper snowflake you make is different—just like every real one is unique.

1 Start with a square piece of paper.

2 Fold this across the diagonal centre to make a triangle.

3 Now fold the triangle in half to make an even smaller triangle.

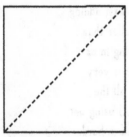

4 With the triangle pointing up (long edge at the bottom) take the left hand edge and fold it so it covers half of the remaining triangle. Then take the right edge and fold it over the rest of the shape.

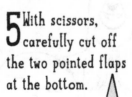

5 With scissors, carefully cut off the two pointed flaps at the bottom.

6 Next snip out little shapes from the two edges of the narrow triangle you have left.

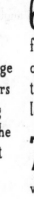

7 Open it out and you'll have your very own snowflake.

Poems

Below are a couple of wacky winter limericks for you to enjoy. Read them out loud for your friends and family.

A toddler, when out on her tricycle,
Encountered a very large icicle;
It poked through the spokes
Till the front wheel broke,
Yet she smiled—she now owned a bicycle!

If a robin's red breast you have sighted,
It's not cos he's hot or excited;
Nor is it a bait
To attract a new mate,
It's because he supports Man United.

Andy Seed

CHRISTMAS MUSIC

Score

What are your favorite Christmas carols? Score these out of ten:

Away in a Manger

Hark the Herald Angels Sing

The Holly and the Ivy

Once in Royal David's City

Ding Dong Merrily on High

Jokes

See if someone can work out these silly jokes based on the classic Christmas carol, The Holly and the Ivy:

What carol should you sing if...

It's raining?	The Brolly and the Ivy
You're at the supermarket?	The Trolley and the Ivy
You like ice cream?	The Lolly and the Ivy
You like playing with Barbie®?	The Dolly and the Ivy
You're a footballer?	The Volley and the Ivy
You're a sheep farmer?	The Collie and the Ivy

Challenges

Merged melodies
Six carols are mixed up here—can you find them?
Answers on page 148.

- God Rest Ye Three Ships
- O Little Merry Gentlemen
- Deck the Town of Bethlehem
- O Come All Ye World
- I Saw Halls
- Joy to the Faithful

Christmas conundrum
Here are three carols, each with their letters jumbled. They are not easy but see if you can work them out.
Answers on page 148.

1. SING LENT HIT

2. SKEW THE REIGN

3. FOR THE SILENT

CHRISTMAS MUSIC

Festive Facts

What do you know about Christmas carols?
Here are some interesting facts.

Christmas carols were banned in England by Oliver Cromwell's government in the seventeenth century. Spoilsports!

Some Christmas carols are over 500 years old. Many of the ones we sing today were written in the 1800s.

At Christmas in 1914, Silent Night was sung together by English and German soldiers during the First World War, even though they were enemies.

The famous story about the mean and nasty Mr. Scrooge, called *A Christmas Carol*, was written by Charles Dickens using a goose quill (a pen made from a feather).

Jingle Bells was actually written to celebrate the American holiday of Thanksgiving, not Christmas! And it was also the first song to be performed in space.

25

Talk

Christmas chart hits

What do you think about Christmas music? Why not ask your friends and family the questions too.

☛ What is your favorite Christmas pop song?

☛ Which is the most annoying Christmas song?

☛ Which Christmas song can't you get out of your head when you hear it?

☛ How good are you at these (score yourself out of ten for each one):
☆ Singing
☆ Playing music
☆ Remembering the words
☆ Staying in tune

Love, hate, or meh?

What's your verdict on these classic hits that are played everywhere, every year?

Last Christmas

I Wish it Could be Christmas Every Day

White Christmas

Winter Wonderland

Rockin' Around the Christmas Tree

Do They Know It's Christmas?

Santa Claus is Comin' to Town

Challenges

It can get a bit boring listening to the same old Christmas songs every year. Why not try changing the words to the song to liven things up? Below is an example to get you started.

We wish you a Merry Christmas;
We wish you a Merry Christmas;
We wish you a Merry Christmas and a Happy New Year.
Good tidings we chat to you and your cat;
We wish you a Merry Christmas and a Happy New Year.

Oh, help us find the gerbil;
Oh, help us find the gerbil;
Oh, help us find the gerbil, we know it's round here.
It might be behind the freezer;
It might be behind the freezer;
It might be behind the freezer, or the cooker—oh dear.

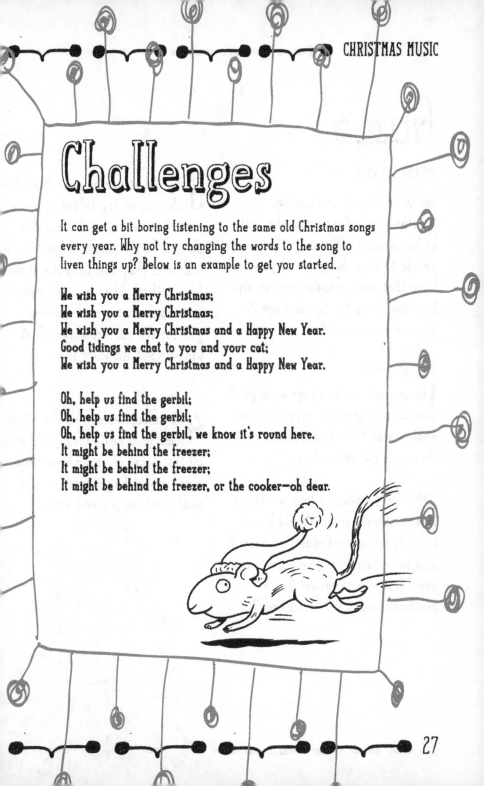

Game

Hummit

Get your friends and family together to find out who's the best at humming! You'll need at least six people to play this game. If you don't have that many people you can still hum the songs for fun and see if anyone can guess them.

HOW TO PLAY:

1 Write each of the songs on page 29 on a small piece of paper (one on each piece), fold them up, and put them in a hat or bowl.

2 Divide the players into two teams. The oldest person should be on team A, the second oldest on team B and so on (why not give your teams some festive nicknames? Santa's Sidekicks or the Christmas Crew?).

3 The oldest person goes first. They take one of the folded pieces of paper but they mustn't show it to anyone (if the person doesn't know the carol they can swap the paper for another). They hum the song they have chosen and whoever guesses the correct answer first wins a point for their team.

4 The oldest person on the other team goes next. Keep going until all the pieces of paper have been used up. Whichever team has the most points at the end wins.

Christmas carols and songs:

If your favorite Christmas songs aren't on this list then just include them! But remember to make sure you have an even number of songs to chose from—otherwise the game won't work!

Angels from the Realms of Glory

Away In a Manger

Deck the Halls

Ding Dong Merrily on High

God Rest Ye Merry Gentlemen

Good King Wenceslas

Hark! The Herald Angels Sing

I Saw Three Ships

In the Bleak Midwinter

It Came Upon a Midnight Clear

Jingle Bells

Joy to the World

O Christmas Tree

O Come, All Ye Faithful

O Little Town Of Bethlehem

Once in Royal David's City

Rudolph the Red-Nose Reindeer

Santa Claus Is Coming To Town

Silent Night

The First Noel

The Holly and the Ivy

Twelve Days of Christmas

We Three Kings of Orient Are

We Wish You a Merry Christmas

White Christmas

Winter Wonderland

Challenges

The Twelve Days of Christmas

Singing the Twelve Days of Christmas is fun, but doing it with some comedy actions is even better! Have a go at these.

On the first day of Christmas, my true love gave to me...

DAY	GIFT	ACTION
1st	Partridge in a pear tree	Join hands over head to make tree shape
2nd	Turtle doves	Bend knees and make small wings with hands down by hips
3rd	French hens	Flap elbows
4th	Calling birds	Make calling action with hands around mouth
5th	Gold rings	Hold up five fingers
6th	Geese-a-laying	Bend knees with bottom out
7th	Swans-a-swimming	Swimming action with arms
8th	Maids-a-milking	Mime milking a cow with hands
9th	Ladies dancing	Hold hand above head and spin round once
10th	Lords-a-leaping	Leap off one foot with one arm up
11th	Pipers piping	Pretend to play pipe
12th	Drummers drumming	Act out drumming

Once you've mastered this challenge, to make it even funnier, try doing them as fast as you can!

Silly Days of Christmas

As well as singing the Twelve Days of Christmas and performing the actions it's good fun to write your own silly version! Have a go at changing the twelve gifts to something completely different.

Here's an example:
- ☉ A cartridge in a spare tea,
- ✪ Two dirty gloves,
- ☉ Three drenched men,
- ✪ Four sprawling burps,
- ☉ Five cold things,

Now make up your own silly version, memorize, and perform it!

Amazing facts

What would happen if someone really got all of the presents in the Twelve D of Christmas? Apart from having a lot of wrapping paper to clean up, this is what you could expect...

On the 12th day of Christmas the true love would receive seventy-eight gifts.

The gifts that the true love would end up with the most of are geese and swans (forty-two of each!).

Over the full twelve days 364 presents would be given.

An American bank makes a calculation every year of how much it would cost to buy or hire all the gifts on the list. In 2015, they would have cost around £24,000.

As well as all the animals, the true love would have to find room for a lot of people (maids, ladies, lords, pipers, and drummers)—140 of them, in fact. I hope they've got a big house!

Ask your friends and family to guess some of the figures above!

Jokes

Carol cackles
Which carol...

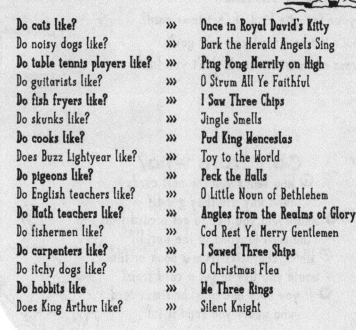

Do cats like?	>>>	Once in Royal David's Kitty
Do noisy dogs like?	>>>	Bark the Herald Angels Sing
Do table tennis players like?	>>>	Ping Pong Merrily on High
Do guitarists like?	>>>	O Strum All Ye Faithful
Do fish fryers like?	>>>	I Saw Three Chips
Do skunks like?	>>>	Jingle Smells
Do cooks like?	>>>	Pud King Wenceslas
Does Buzz Lightyear like?	>>>	Toy to the World
Do pigeons like?	>>>	Peck the Halls
Do English teachers like?	>>>	O Little Noun of Bethlehem
Do Math teachers like?	>>>	Angles from the Realms of Glory
Do fishermen like?	>>>	Cod Rest Ye Merry Gentlemen
Do carpenters like?	>>>	I Sawed Three Ships
Do itchy dogs like?	>>>	O Christmas Flea
Do hobbits like	>>>	We Three Rings
Does King Arthur like?	>>>	Silent Knight

CHRISTMAS CARDS
Talk

Card kinds
❷ What's your favorite kind of Christmas card?
⊙ What's the best card you ever got?
❷ Which types of Christmas cards don't you like?

Ooh, from who?
⊙ Who sends you the best cards
(and why are they good)?
❸ Who would you like to get a card from
the most (anyone in the world)?
⊙ Which character from a book or film
would you like to get a card from?
❸ If you only had one Christmas card,
who would you send it to?

Score

Your kind of card?

Rate these types of Christmas cards by giving them a score out of ten:

* Glittery
* Homemade
* Old-fashioned snow scenes
* Nativity cards

* Pop-ups
* Unusual shapes
* Jokes
* Cartoons

* Homemade cards
* Robins
* Angels
* Santa
* Christmas trees
* Photos of people

Advent calendars

Put these in order of how much you like them (1 = favourite):

* Simple card windows showing pictures inside
* Hanging cloth calendar with little pockets
* Personalized scratch calendar
* Wooden house calendar with windows
* Box calendar with chocolates inside
* Crazy homemade design

Challenges

In the past nearly every Christmas card used to have a cheesy verse inside. You can have fun with these by changing some of the words.

Try changing the underlined words in this one:

A special <u>wish</u> is being sent
Just for you today,
Filled with all the <u>Christmas joy</u>
That's sure to come your way.

> EXAMPLE:
> A special pie is being sent
> Just for you today,
> Filled with all the monkey brains
> That's sure to come your way.

Here's another one to try:

A time of hope, a time of <u>peace,</u>
A time for everyone,
To join together <u>happily</u>
For <u>presents</u>, food, and fun.

Mixed up in the post

Can you unscramble these anagrams to find things you'll find in the Christmas post?

⊙ OVENPEEL
⊙ MAPS TON
⊙ INERT EGG
⊙ DART RICH SCAMS
⊙ STRAPS MISMATCH

Answers on page 148.

Choose

Who would you rather get a Christmas card from?

David Beckham or the Queen?
Rihanna or Harry Styles?
Elvis or Henry VIII?
Batman or Spider Man?
Harry Potter or James Bond?
An alien or Godzilla?
Now make up some pairs of your own
to ask a friend.

Tom Smith
34, High Street
Lower Upper
LO34 9RS

Sadly, Christmas cards are being sent less
often as people post greetings over the Internet.
Pick which one of these you'd rather receive instead of a card:

▶ A video message from granny

▶ An animated e-card from cousin Dwayne

▶ A photo slideshow from Uncle Gunter

▶ A twinkly Tweet from Auntie Morag

Get creative

Design some new stamps

New Christmas stamps are issued each year—but are they as fun as the ones you would create? Here's your chance to put your own 'stamp' on Christmas.

Rudolph
Santa's Sleigh
Row One
The Sky

Fun facts

Postal problems

The Royal Mail delivers millions of Christmas cards each year and most of them have the correct address. However, some of them don't have any addresses at all, some have handwriting on them that is so bad it can't be read, and then there are the senders who just don't know the addresses at all...

One card was addressed to:
Bill and Mary,
The Big White House with the double garage,
[Name of village]

Another address was:
Mr McFee,
Glasgow
There are quite a few Mr McFees in Glasgow so this probably didn't arrive. One with more of a clue was this one:
Mrs T Johnson,
A road somewhere near a golf course,
[Name of town]
Amazingly, that one did arrive!

So did this one, because the clever postman worked it out:
Miss Smith,
The House with the blue door,
[Town]

One frequent letter sender likes to test the postmen and women each year by making her addresses into a kind of puzzle. Once she sent an address in mirror writing. Another time she created a crossword on the envelope so that the postman had to solve the clues to work out the address. It arrived on time!

If you do send cards by post, remember always to use the postcode or they might never arrive!

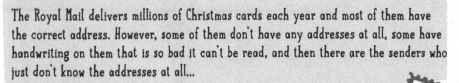

Guess

Get your family and friends to guess these facts and figures about Christmas cards—the nearest wins.

What is the average number of Christmas cards bought by people in the UK each year?
(About thirty each)

What is the total number of Christmas cards bought in the UK each year?
(About 884 million)

What year was the first Christmas card sent?
(1843)

How much money is spent on Christmas cards in the UK each year?
(£130 million)

How much money is raised by charities in the UK each year by selling Christmas cards?
(£50 million)

How many Christmas cards are sent in the USA each year?
(Three billion)

How much was the most expensive Christmas card bought at auction?
(£20,000—paid in 2000 for one of the world's earliest Christmas cards, sent in 1843)

Get creative

How to make a pop-up Christmas card

Pop-up cards can be much more exciting than a plain old flat card and there are lots of simple ways to make one.

Below are some instructions for a basic pop-up Christmas tree. Practice with some scrap paper to get the hang of what to do.

1 Fold a rectangular piece of paper or card in half.

2 Draw a triangle along the folded edge:

3 Draw four dotted lines on your triangle as shown here. With scissors, cut along the four dotted lines.

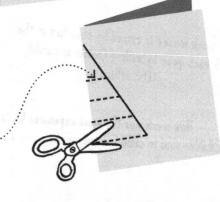

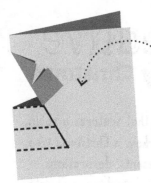

4 You should now have four flaps. Lift each flap and fold it down against the solid line of the triangle.

5 Turn the paper over and repeat this fold the other way for each flap.

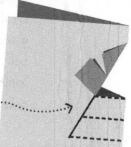

6 Now open the folded rectangle and fold it the other way (back along the same center crease).

7 Then partly open the fold and push the four folded flaps through the center so they stick out. Press the card down—you should now see a pop-up Christmas tree shape.

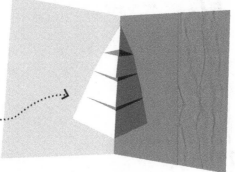

8 Color and decorate the tree in any way you like!

9 To finish, stick your pop-up Christmas tree inside another piece of folded card.

Get creative

Design a busy Christmas card

Create a Christmas card that features a robin, a snowman, a star, a turkey, a Christmas tree, holly, bells, candles, presents, decorations, Santa, a reindeer, elves, a stocking, a Christmas cake, angels, and wise men!

Mini-quiz

Are you a Christmas card nut?

Take this quiz to find out....

1. When do you start writing Christmas cards?
a) Early December
b) November
c) January

2. Who do you send Christmas cards to?
a) Close family
b) All my friends
c) Everyone I know (plus a few people I don't know just for fun)

3. How much do you spend on cards?
a) About £5
b) About £20
c) It has lots of zeros!

4. What do you write in the cards?
a) Just my name
b) A bit of news
c) Everything that happened during the year (including haircuts)

5. Where do you put the Christmas cards that people send to you?
a) On shelves
b) Across the walls
c) On display all year round

6. What do you do with old cards?
a) Recycle them
b) Keep them
c) Wallpaper the house with them, of course!

What your answers mean:

Mostly 'A's:
You're definitely not a Christmas card nut.

Mostly 'B's:
You're keen and it's smiles all round.

Mostly 'C's:
Hmmm, I think you are overdoing it slightly... I'm lying, you're overdoing it A LOT!

Feathered facts

Robins

Robins feature on a huge number of Christmas cards every year. Here are ten fun facts about these special little birds:

1. Robins were voted the UK's favourite bird in a 2015 poll.
2. There are over six million robins in Britain.
3. The robin is one of the very few birds that sings all year round.
4. Both male and female robins have red breasts.
5. An old name for the robin is the ruddock.
6. Robins eat spiders, insects, worms, berries, fruit, seeds, and anything on a bird table.
7. Robins are less afraid of people than most birds and will even eat out of a person's hand sometimes.
8. Robins occasionally make their nests in strange places in gardens such as in watering cans or barbecues!
9. An adult robin weighs about the same as two one-pound coins.
10. Early postmen were called 'robins' because they wore red uniforms.

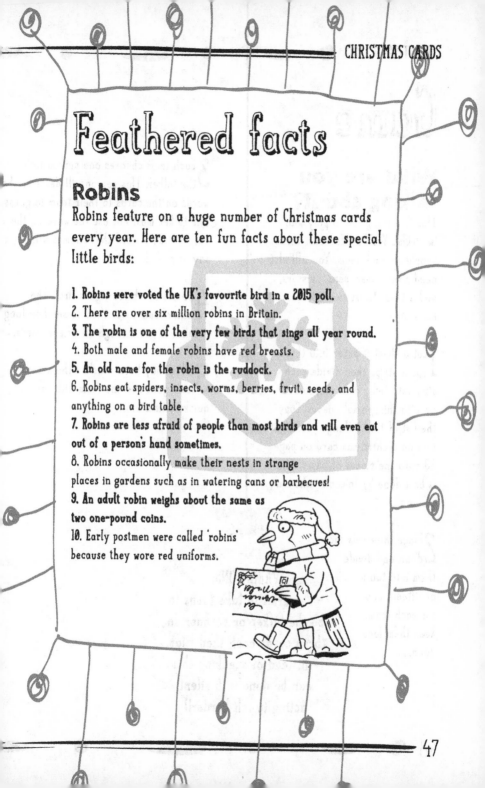

Game

What are you talking about?

This is a fun game to play with two teams. You'll need at least three people on each team. You will also need some paper, pens, scissors, and a timer (most smartphones have one).

1 Cut a sheet of paper into three equal strips then divide each strip into ten pieces so you end up with thirty small pieces. Copy the list of thirty things you might find on a Christmas card on page 49 onto the pieces of paper. This is best done by someone who isn't playing.

2 Place the cards face down and divide them into two piles of fifteen, one for each team. Keep them face down.

3 Each team chooses one person to be the talker. This person will describe the words on the cards to their team to guess. The talker must not use the word on the card or say a word that rhymes with it or say any of the letters in it.

4 Decide which team goes first. The other team times them to see how long it takes to get through all fifteen cards.

5 After they have finished the second team goes and the team with the quickest time wins.

VARIATIONS:

• Players can take turns to be the talker or perhaps do three cards each then swap.
• Instead of speaking this can be done with silent acting (much harder!)

Thirty things you might find on a Christmas card

Snowflake	Stocking	Sleigh
Baby Jesus	Donkey	Present
Advent calendar	Elf	Fairy lights
Carol singer	Angel	Sprouts
Reindeer	Bauble	Christmas pudding
Holly	Father Christmas	Shepherd
Star	Robin	Mince pie
Candle	Wise men	Santa
Turkey	Christmas tree	Mary
Christmas cracker	Snowman	Bell

TREES AND DECORATIONS

Talk

Have a nattery chat with someone to see if their tastes match yours.

Trees and tinsel

* What are your favorite Christmas decorations?
* If you could have your own Christmas tree how would you decorate it? It can be as wacky as you like!
* Which do you prefer, real Christmas trees or fake ones? Give a reason for your answer.

Bright lights

* If you owned a house would you cover it in Christmas lights outside? How many would you have?
* What's the best display of lights you've ever seen?

Choose

Which decorations do you prefer?

Tinsel or Christmas lights?
Door wreaths or Christmas bunting?
Chocolate or gingerbread decorations?

Star on top of the tree or fairy?
Baubles or felt characters?
Silver or gold ornaments?

Challenge

Jumbled up decorations

Ten Christmas decoration names have been jumbled up.
Can you rearrange the letters to discover what they are?
The answers are on page 148.

1. RATS
2. YOHLL
3. INLETS
4. YARIF
5. WATHER

6. LUBBEA
7. KINGCOTS
8. LANCED
9. DRANGAL
10. SNOBRIB

Can you come up with your own Christmas decoration anagrams for your friends and family to solve? Below are a few decorations for you to jumble up to get you started:

Bell

Snowman

Angel

Ribbon

Reindeer

Deco-rate
Rate each of the following out of ten.

Love, hate, or meh?
Give your verdict on these traditional, old-school decorations.

Real Christmas tree

Silver Christmas tree

Tree with flashing lights

Tree with coloured lights

LED reindeer   Inflatable Santa

Hanging icicle lights

'Santa stop here' signs

Giant illuminated garden snowman

Paper chains

Stockings

Hanging paper

Bell

Holly

Crib with nativity scene

Ribbons

Jokes

Most people put fairy lights on their Christmas tree but...

What do the following put on their tree?

Cows	**Dairy lights**
Gorillas	Hairy lights
Yellow birds	**Canary lights**
Cowboys	Prairie lights
Dracula	**Scary lights**
Joseph	Mary lights

A few groaners

Why are Christmas trees no good at knitting?
They keep losing their needles.

What do you get if you eat Christmas decorations?
Tinselitis.

Why are fairies grumpy at Christmas?
You would be too if you had a tree stuck up your bottom.

Get Creative

Here's a chance to decorate a tree in exactly the way YOU want.

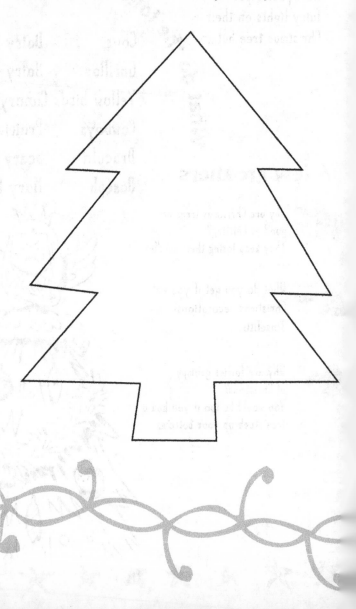

Make this one REALLY different. Maybe hang
multi-colored socks from the branches?

Guess

Ask a group of people to guess these
Christmas tree facts and see who
gets closest to the right answer.

**How many Christmas trees are
sold in the UK each year?**
(Around six million)

**Roughly how many people in
Britain are injured each year
by Christmas trees?**
(Around 750)

**Where did Christmas trees
come in a survey of Britain's
favorite smells?**
(Eighth)

**How tall was the tallest ever
cut Christmas tree in meters?**
(Sixty-seven meters)

**What year did the first
Christmas tree appear in
the UK?**
(1841)

**For each tree cut down how
many young trees are planted?**
(Three)

Amazing facts

House lights madness!

In 2013 the Richards family in Canberra, Australia, set a new world record for the most lights on a house, with 518,838 lights (that's over half a million). It had over forty-eight kilometers of LED string lights and the electricity bill was around £1400 for one month!

However, the record was broken in 2014 by the Gay family from New York who put 601,736 lights around their home. They are now sponsored by a famous cracker company and have so many lights covering their home that you can't actually see the house any more!

In one Christmas-crazy home in Norfolk, UK, even the toilet gets decked out with lights and decorations at Christmas.

In Hedge End, Hampshire, UK, a whole street is lit up with spectacular lights. The residents there have raised over £38,000 for a local children's hospital.

However, all of these bright lights aren't all fun and cheer for everyone. In some cases neighbors have stopped talking to people who combine bright lights with loud Christmas music each night... Whoops.

<<<<<<<<

Get creative
Star decoration

Lots of people hang stars on their trees at Christmas. Use the instructions below to make your own star to hang on your tree.

YOU WILL NEED:
- A cardboard tube
- Glue
- Glitter
- Scissors
- Thread
- Five clothes pegs

WHAT TO DO:

1 Press down on the card tube so that it becomes flat.

2 Measure two centimeters from the bottom of the tube and cut across it so you end up with a petal shape.

3 Do this five times and arrange the pieces of card into a star shape.

4 Next, glue all five pieces together where they touch and hold them together with pegs while the glue dries.

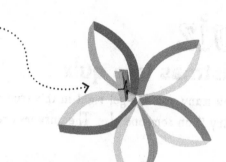

5 Once the pieces of card are well and truly stuck together, coat the entire star (inside and out) with glue. Use a brush to do this. While the glue is still wet, sprinkle glitter over each surface.

6 Once the glue and glitter have set, tie a loop of thread onto the star and hang it from your Christmas tree.

Quiz
Christmas tree quiz

See how many you can get right in this true or false quiz.
Then try it on someone else. The answers are on page 149.

1. The first Christmas
trees were put up in China.

2. It takes around five years to grow
a two-meter fir tree.

3. The large Christmas tree that stands in Trafalgar
Square, London each year is a gift from Norway.
It is to thank the British people for their
help during World War II.

4. Before fairy lights were invented,
real candles were put on Christmas trees.

5. Each December the President of the USA lights
The National Christmas Tree outside The White House
in America.

6. A one-meter-tall spruce tree has over one million
needles.

Lists

Good and bad things to hang on a Christmas tree

GOOD	BAD
Baubles	Bubbles
Angels	Mangels
Tinsel	Tonsils
Ribbons and bows	Gibbons and cows
Bells	Bulls
Snowflakes	Snotflakes

Can you add any more ideas to this silly list?

Games

O dear

Play this game and see how weird and wacky some Christmas decorations start to sound!

- **Think up a list of Christmas decorations.**
- Change all the vowels in the word to the letter 'o'.
- **For example, if the word is 'gingerbread' it will then become, 'gongorbrood'.**
- See who can come up with the funniest new word.
- **Try using another vowel too.**

Decorations dialogue

See who's the Christmas decorations expert!

HOW TO PLAY:
- You will need two or more people.
- **Take turns to name different Christmas decorations.**
- The first person to be stuck is out.
- **You can have any kind of decoration: tree ornaments, types of lights, natural objects used at Christmas, paper decorations, shapes commonly used (stars, bells etc.), and more.**

- To make it more challenging you can change the rules slightly so that each word must start with the last letter of the previous word. For example:
  o Person A says, 'holly'
  o Person B says, 'yule log'
  o Person A says, 'glitter'
  o Person B says, 'reindeer', and so on...

Jokes

Christmas tree typo trouble

If you're writing to someone about your Christmas tree plans this year, make sure you get your spelling write...

RIGHT	WRONG
We're having a fir tree this year.	We're having a fur tree this year.
Aunt Myrtle likes a larch in her hall.	Aunt Myrtle likes a lurch in her hall.
The Scots pine looks great next to the TV.	The Scots pie looks great next to the TV.
Dad can just about fit a cypress in the lounge.	Dad can just about fit Cyprus in the lounge.
I prefer an artificial tree with flashing lights.	I prefer an artificial tree with flashing tights.

THAT MAN SANTA

Choose

Imagine that you are Santa Claus. Would you rather...
Eat mince pies or cookies?
Climb down chimneys or live at the North Pole?
Look after reindeer or train elves?
Deliver thousands of presents or sit in a warm grotto?
Fly in a sleigh or appear in films?
Read funny children's letters or only work one night a year?

Jokes

Q. What goes 'Oh oh oh?'
A. Santa walking backwards.

Q. Why doesn't Father Christmas have a job?
A. One of the elves gave him the sack.

Q. Where does Father Christmas go on holiday?
A. A ho-ho-tel.

Q. What language does Santa Claus speak?
A. North Polish.

Q. What do the elves say to Santa when he's calling the register?
A. Present.

Q. What is Rudolph's favorite time of the year?
A. Red Nose Day.

Get creative

Letters to Santa are fun to write. Here's one for you to fill in (or you can copy it out):

Dear Santa,

This year I have been very good / quite good / OK / a bit naughty / a total horror.

For Christmas I would like a small / medium / big / massive present.

I am hoping that I will get (circle):

A pair of socks

A cuddly rabbit

A basketball

A radio-controlled car

A train set

A computer

A new bike

A drum kit

A new phone

A ride-on hovercraft

A pet tiger

My own tropical island

And also I'd like a _____

I have left you some crumbs / biscuits / mince pies / turkey dinner / gourmet food hamper.

Love, _____

Lists

Santa has lots of different names all around the world.
Here are just a few of them.

Brazil–Papai Noel
Netherlands–Kerstman
Finland–Joulupukki
France–Pere Noel
Germany–Weihnachtsmann
Italy–Babbo Natale
Norway–Julenissen
Poland–Swiety Mikolaj
Russia–Ded Moroz
South Africa–Sinterklaas
Sweden–Jultomten
United Kingdom–Father Christmas
USA–Kris Kringle (and Santa Claus, of course!)

Challenge

The Rev Spooner's list for Santa

The Reverend William Archibald Spooner taught students at Oxford University over a hundred years ago. He was famous for muddling up his words when he spoke. If you've ever come out with 'par cark' when you meant to say 'car park', you're doing what Spooner used to do.

Here is a made up (and mixed up) list of presents for Santa. See if you can work out what they are.

The answers are on page 149.

1. coy tar
2. bootfall foots
3. beddy tear
4. boom lands
5. roy tobot
6. puinea gig
7. cooker snue
8. trumper duck
9. pigsaw juzzle
10. dobot rog
11. phobile mone
12. sainting pet

Can you make up some more to add to the list?

Fun facts

According to the Royal Mail, Santa's official address is:
Santa's Grotto,
Reindeerland,
XM4 5HQ

There is a Santa Claus Post Office in Northern Finland which receives letters addressed to Father Christmas at the North Pole—it gets over 500,000 letters to Santa each year!

It's reported that children from Italy write the most letters to Santa.

In order to get a reply, letters to Santa should be posted by Dec 6th (don't forget to include a stamped, addressed envelope).

Santa can be tracked online each Christmas Eve via the NORAD (North American Air Defence) website! Google also has a Santa tracker.

Quiz
Reindeer quiz

How much do you really know about reindeer? Ask your friends and family too and see how many they get right.

1. Which of the following is correct: 'two reindeers' or 'two reindeer'?
2. What is the other name for a reindeer: caribou or moose?
3. True or false: reindeer grow a new set of antlers every year.
4. A large male reindeer weighs the same as roughly how many adult humans?
5. True or false: reindeer knees click when they walk.
6. Reindeer form large groups of up to half a million animals when they migrate—what are these called?
7. True or false: baby reindeer can't run.
8. Which of these predators does NOT hunt reindeer: wolves, bears, eagles, crocodiles, wolverines.
9. Which reindeer in a story has a red nose?
10. What is the missing name in this list of the reindeer that traditionally pull Santa's sleigh? Dasher, Dancer, Prancer, Vixen, Comet, Cupid, Donner, and ____?

The answers are on page 149.

Score

There are lots of puns about Santa's elves and most of them are terrible!
Give each of these elf jokes a score by circling the stars below:

❄ Arrrrgghhh!
❄ ❄ Made me groan.
❄ ❄ ❄ I nearly smiled.
❄ ❄ ❄ ❄ Chuckled a bit.
❄ ❄ ❄ ❄ ❄ Laughed my head off.

What do you call a very small rock star?
Elfis.
❄ ❄ ❄ ❄ ❄

What do you call a rich elf?
Welfy.
❄ ❄ ❄ ❄ ❄

Where do elves get fit?
On an elf farm.
❄ ❄ ❄ ❄ ❄

What's the first thing elves learn at school?
The elfabet.
❄ ❄ ❄ ❄ ❄

What do elves do with their smartphones?
Take elfies.
❄ ❄ ❄ ❄ ❄

Get creative
Sleek sleigh

Let's face it, Santa's sleigh is a bit of a rickety, old-school mode of transport. Here's your chance to sleek it up and create the Ferrari of the sled world.

Speed boosters

Tech improvements

Go faster stripes

Fun gadgets

Anything else that adds style, speed, and wow

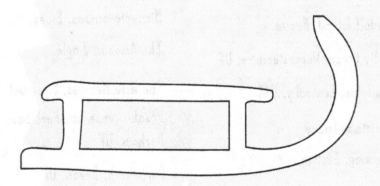

Lists

Santa stops here?

Here are some real places that are just made for Santa (and some silly ones that are not):

REAL	NOT REAL
Bethlehem, Pennsylvania, USA	Sprout City, California, USA
Santa Claus, Indiana, USA	Hohohoton, Kent, UK
Christmas, Florida, USA	Snowmanchester, UK
Noel, Missouri, USA	Unwanted Gift, Ohio, USA
Rudolf Island, Russia	Mincepie-on-Sea, Essex, UK
Holly Green, Worcestershire, UK	The Amazon Jingle
Mistletoe, Kentucky, USA	The Wise Mendips, Somerset, UK
Christmas Island	Frankincense-on-the-Elbow, Durham, UK
Stocking, Austria	Dartmyrrh, Devon, UK
Turkey!	

Guess
The North Pole

Santa is supposed to live at the North Pole—but how much do you know about the real North Pole? It's fun to guess these tricky answers with other people and see who is the nearest.

The answers are on page 150.

1. On average, how thick is the ice at the North Pole (in meters)?
2. The North Pole is in the middle of the Arctic Ocean. How deep is the sea at the North Pole (in meters)?
3. What year did an explorer first reach the North Pole?
4. What is the average winter temperature at the North Pole (in degrees Celsius)?
5. How many countries have lands within the Arctic Circle?

Challenge

How many words of two or more letters can you make out of the letters in:

There are some answers on page 150.

SLEIGH BELLS

TARGETS
10 words: OK
15 words: good
20 words: wow
30 words: genius!

Get Creative
How to draw Santa

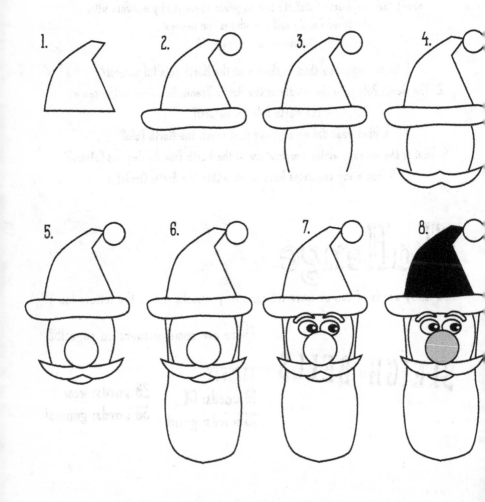

YIPPEE: PRESENTS!

Talk

Present and correct

- What are the best two presents you've ever had?
- What's the best present you've ever given anyone?
- What's the worst present you've ever received?

Imagine

- If you could buy each person at home anything at all, what would you choose and why?
- Which famous person would you like to buy a present for and what would you buy?

Choose

Pick which present you'd prefer.

- Book or torch?
- DVD or trainers?
- Walkie talkie or telescope?
- Roller blades or scooter?
- Remote control helicopter or popcorn maker?
- Drum kit or snooker table?
- Camera or clothes?
- Hexbug or Cluedo?

Jokes

Rhyming gifts

What present should you give to people with these jobs?

For an actor? A purple tractor...
For a farmer? A suit of armor...
For a vet? A private jet...
For a graphic designer? A trip to China...
For a truck driver? A brand new fiver...
For a spy? Some sausage pie...
For a waiter? A small alligator...
For an illustrator? A cheese grater...
For a nurse? Some nonsense verse...
For a banker? An oil tanker...

Try adding some more to the list. What would you buy...

For a cook?
For an engineer?
For a security guard?
For a tour guide?
For a coal miner?
For a chef?
For a company boss?
For a chimney sweep
For a singer?
For a _____

Lists
Wacky stuff you can buy

There are hundreds of gifts on the Internet. Thousands. Millions. And most of them are OK but some of them are definitely out of the ordinary!

Potty Putting
This is a mini golf game you play sitting on the toilet.

Bacon flavored toothpaste
Need I say more? It's bacon flavored toothpaste.

Dog umbrella
This attaches to a dog lead, leaving your pooch dry and confused...

Runny nose shower dispenser
This is a large plastic nose fitted to your shower tiles that dispenses gel when you press it. Nice!

Backwards clock
The numbers on this clock are in the reverse order and the hands go backwards—guaranteed to never get you anywhere on time!

Chocolate pizza
It's exactly what it sounds like—a pizza made of chocolate: you dreamt about it and now somebody's made it.

Poo pen
Well, basically it's a pen in the shape of a poo. And yes, you can really buy one.

Games

Shop until you drop out

Everyone tries to shop for the perfect gift at Christmas! Here is a shopping list memory game for a group of three or more people.

HOW TO PLAY:

* Each player starts by saying, 'I went to the shops and I bought...' then adds an item.
* You can buy anything at all, no matter how wacky!
* The next player repeats what the first person bought then adds his or her own item.
* This carries on with players taking turns, repeating all the items in order then adding one more.
* The first player to forget an item or get stuck is out.

EXAMPLE:

* Player 1: "I went to the shops and bought a spade."
* Player 2: "I went to the shops and bought a spade and some submarines."
* Player 3: "I went to the shops and bought a spade, some submarines, and two owls."
* And so on...

If you want to make the game harder, get each player to say who the present is for.

Alphabet presents

This is similar to the 'shop until you drop' game but a bit easier because it uses the alphabet.

HOW TO PLAY:

* The game is for any group of three or more people, who all take turns.
* The first player says, "A is for..." (and names a gift beginning with A)
  * The second person says, "A is for...., and B is for... (and names a gift starting with B)

FOR EXAMPLE:

* Player 1: "A is for alarm clock."
* Player 2: "A is for alarm clock and B is for baby rattle."
* Player 3: "A is for alarm clock and B is for baby rattle, and C is for cheese."
* And so on...

Score

Rate each of the presents below with a score out of ten:

Scalextric™   Rapidough   Glitter tattoo set

Guitar   Socks   Chemistry set   Monopoly

Onesie   Walkie talkie   Bike

Love, hate or meh?
What's your verdict on each of these presents?

Rubik's Cube   Watercolor paints   Table football

Kite   Yo-yo   Model train   Magic set   TV

Challenge

Perfect present or grotty gift?

Decide who's the best person to receive each of these presents and who's the worst! The first has been done for you. Add a couple of your own gift ideas at the end.

Present:	Best person to give it to:	Worst person to give it to:
Aftershave	Uncle Peter	My little sister
Karaoke machine		
Trampoline		
Santa outfit		
Make-up set		
Darts and dartboard		
Tablet computer		
Chocolate fountain		

Poems

How about it, Santa?

Dear Santa,

For Christmas this year
I'd like:
Peace on Earth,
An end to all violence,
Enough food for the starving millions,
1000 new hospitals,
Love between all races...

And an iPad.

P.S.
Don't worry if you can't manage
All the peace and love stuff.

Andy Seed

Doctor Who at Christmas

What shall I buy for a Dalek?
A woolly hat would look pleasant;
Or a voucher to go to the future or
past?
No, I think I'll stick with the present.

Andy Seed

Christmas Plea

For Christmas this year you can give me
A pack of moldy cheese,
A pair of broken roller skates,
An ugly cat with fleas.

For Christmas this year I'd be happy to get
Some bath oil that smells of fish,
An ill-fitting, bad-taste jumper,
A second-hand butter dish.

For Christmas this year it would be lovely to have
A jigsaw minus the box,
A scratched CD by a rubbish band,
Anything
But
SOCKS!

Andy Seed

Lists
Top toys

Every January, the British Association of Toy Retailers announces its Toy of the Year. Here are some of the winners through the years:

YEAR	WINNING TOY
1965	James Bond Aston Martin Car
1966	Action Man
1967	Spirograph
1970	Sindy® Doll
1974	Lego®
1977	Playpeople by Playmobil®
1980	Rubik's Cube
1985	Transformers
1988	Sylvanian Families®
1991	Nintendo® Game Boy
1994	Power Rangers
1995	Pogs
1997	Teletubbies
1998	Furby
2004	Robosapien
2009	Go Go Hamsters
2010	Jet Pack Buzz Lightyear
2013	Teksta Robotic Puppy
2014	Disney Frozen Snow Glow Elsa
2015	Pie Face

Mini-quiz

How good are you at buying Christmas presents?

Take this quiz yourself and find out!

1. What would you buy for your bald uncle?
a) A book by his favorite author
b) A pirate hat
c) A comb

2. What would you buy for next-door's baby?
a) A cute bath toy
b) Car racing gloves
c) A barbecue set

3. What would you buy for your great granny?
a) A necklace
b) Chewing gum
c) A surfboard

4. What would you buy for a cat?
a) Some fish chunks
b) Crayons
c) Minecraft

5. What would you buy the Queen?
a) Corgi food
b) A set of darts
c) A whoopee cushion

What your scores mean:

Mostly 'A's:
Top marks! You will bring everyone smiles this Christmas!

Mostly 'B's:
Hmmmm, I think it might be best to take advice from others when you go shopping.

Mostly 'C's:
Yikes! Don't spend any money on presents—it will be a complete waste!

Get creative
Make some gift tags

Sparkle up your Christmas presents with homemade gift tags. Here are some ideas to get you started.

1 RECYCLED CHRISTMAS CARDS

If you have kept some old Christmas cards, you can cut out parts of the front to make simple gift tags. Make sure there's no writing behind the picture. Use a hole punch to make a hole and attach a loop of thin bright ribbon.

2 DECORATED PLAIN CARD TAGS

If you have some plain card, white or colored, you can cut it into gift tags then decorate them in a variety of ways:

☞ Use a gold or silver pen to make simple repeated patterns like swirls, stars, dots, snowfla or zig-zags.

☞ Star stickers in shiny foil are a neat and ea way to give your gift tags some zing.

☞ Glue and glitter is another way to add spar

3 **STITCH A SIMPLE DESIGN**
If you're handy with a needle and thread then you can add a simple design to a plain card tag by sewing. Choose an easy pattern such as a star like the one below. Go for Christmas colors like red and green or gold.

4 **DRAW IT**
Draw a miniature Christmas scene on paper, add some color, cut it out carefully, then stick it onto a card tag to make something really special for someone.

Challenge

Present-giving around the world

Here are some things that people say when giving and receiving gifts. But can you match the languages to the right translation? Some are easy, some are hard... (Punctuation has been removed.)

1. "Hooray socks again"

2. "Happy Christmas granny"

3. "Thank you, these are unusual"

4. "Just what I've always wanted"
5. "Did you keep the receipt"

6. "I made it myself"

7. "They didn't have your size"

A. "Dank u deze ongewone" (Dutch)

B. "Justo lo que siempre he querido" (Spanish)

C. "Rinne mé é mé féin" (Irish)

D. "Evviva calzini di nuovo" (Italian)

E. "Ich habe es selbst gemacht" (German)

F. "non in magnitudine tua" (Latin)

G. "Joyeux noël mamie" (French)

Answers on page 150.

Games
Twenty Questions

This game is best played with a group of three or more people although it is possible to play it with just two. You don't need anything at all—just your brain!

HOW TO PLAY:

* Decide who's going to go first. That player thinks of a present (but doesn't tell anyone what it is).
* The other players then try to work out the mystery item by asking questions.
* Players can only ask questions which can be answered with a yes or no.
* Only twenty questions are allowed for each round. If no one guesses by the end of the twenty questions then the person answering questions is the winner.
* Remember to keep count of the questions asked, otherwise you won't know when the game finishes.
* If someone guesses the present, then that player gets to go next.

FOR EXAMPLE:

* Player 1 thinks of a cookery book and says 'ready'.
* Player 2 asks, 'Is it a useful item?' (Answer: Yes)
* Player 3 asks, 'Do you own one?' (Answer: No because Player 1 doesn't like cooking!)
* Player 2 asks, 'Can you eat it?' (Answer: No)
* Player 3 asks, 'Is there one in this house?' (Answer: Yes)
* And so on.

Challenges

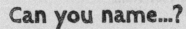

Can you name...?

1. Four presents beginning with M for children?
2. Five presents made of glass?
3. Three shops beginning with B?
4. Ten gifts beginning with C for adults?

Some answers are on page 150.

Odd one out

Below are some different places that Christmas presents
are left around the world. But which one is made up?
The answer is on page 151.

- In shoes
- Under a tree
- In stockings hung up

- In boots
- In the bath
- In pillow cases

Fun facts

Palace presents

Her Majesty The Queen and other members of the royal family are often given presents. Here are some of the strangest gifts they've been given (all true!):

A cheetah
This was given to King George III by India in 1764.

Five hundred tins of pineapple
These were sent to Buckingham Palace by the American government in 1947 to ease rationing.

A thirty meter totem pole
The people of Canada gave this to the Queen in 1958.

A pair of cowboy boots
Presented to The Queen during a visit to the USA in 1991.

A whale tooth
This was sent to the Royal family by Fiji's prime minister in 1997.

A chocolate coach
Donated by Mars to the Queen in 2013.

A book called *Your Arms Remind Me of Pork Luncheon Meat*
Given to Princess Anne in 2013.

A newborn crocodile
Given to baby Prince George (although he won't get to see it much—it will carry on living at Crocosaurus Cove, a zoo in Darwin, Australia!)

YUM YUM, CHRISTMAS DINNER

Talk

Find out what your friends and family like most about Christmas dinner. Do they have the same taste as you?

Dinner delights and disasters

• What's your perfect Christmas dinner?
• What's your favorite part of Christmas dinner?
• What's your least favorite part of Christmas dinner?

Treat and eats

• Apart from Christmas dinner, what are your top festive treats to eat?
• If you could invite two famous people to Christmas dinner, who would you choose?
• What would you serve them? A traditional Christmas meal or something completely weird and wacky?

Amazing facts

There is a mince pie eating contest held each year at Wookey Hole in the UK. Here are some facts about it...

• The record for the most mince pies eaten was set in 2006 when Sonya Thomas ate forty-six of them!
• The contestants are given just ten minutes to eat as many as possible.
• In 2011 the winner received £1000 prize money.
• In 2008 Andy Tree finished last: he ate no pies!

Score

Rate these Christmas dinner foods out of ten, and find out how your scores compare to others:

Roast potatoes

Swede   Mashed potatoes

Chestnut stuffing

Sprouts   Parsnips

Pigs in blankets (mini sausages wrapped in bacon)

Yorkshire puddings   Sage and onion stuffing

Red cabbage   Peas   Bread sauce

Roast turkey   Cranberry sauce

Carrots   Gravy

Fun facts

Here are some curious things about Christmas dinner that you might like to know.

☞ Ripe fresh cranberries will bounce if you drop them!

☞ Before turkey, the traditional Christmas dinner in many British homes was a pig's head and mustard.

☞ An old tradition is to put a silver coin in a Christmas pudding for someone to find.

☞ Mince pies used to contain a mixture of fruit and meat.

☞ In 2014 a man called Stuart Kettell pushed a sprout up the highest mountain in Wales, Mount Snowden, using just his nose! It took him four days.

☞ According to Guinness World Records, the largest Christmas dinner on sale is served by a pub in Worcestershire called the Duck Inn. It consists of a whole turkey, 175 trimmings, and a pint of gravy. Anyone who manages to eat the nearly-ten-kilogram meal gets a T-shirt. Although it probably won't fit...

Get Creative

Design your own Christmas Menu

Fed up with soggy sprouts, cold gravy, and lumpy mashed potatoes?
Well here's your chance to create your own special Christmas menu!
Choose an imaginative starter, a spectacular main course and a
truly original dessert. And don't forget a fancy drink!

∽ Starter ∾

∽ Main Course ∾

∽ Dessert ∾

∽ To Drink ∾

Choose

Pick which sweet thing you'd go for in each pair:
Christmas cake or **chocolate coins?**
Selection box or **chocolate tree decorations?**
Nuts or **satsumas?**
Mince pies or **Christmas pudding?**
Chocolate sauce or **trifle?**
Marzipan fruits or **gingerbread treats?**

Challenge

Typo tee hee

Sometimes when a menu is written down spelling mistakes or typos
(typing goofs) are included by accident. The results can be very funny!
In the Christmas dinner menu below, change one letter from each item to make it sound as
wacky as possible!

ITEM	EXAMPLE	YOUR IDEA
roast turkey	goast turkey	
mashed potatoes	masked potatoes	
stuffing	scuffing	
peas	pets	
bread sauce	dread sauce	
Christmas pudding	Christmas padding	
mince pies	mince ties	

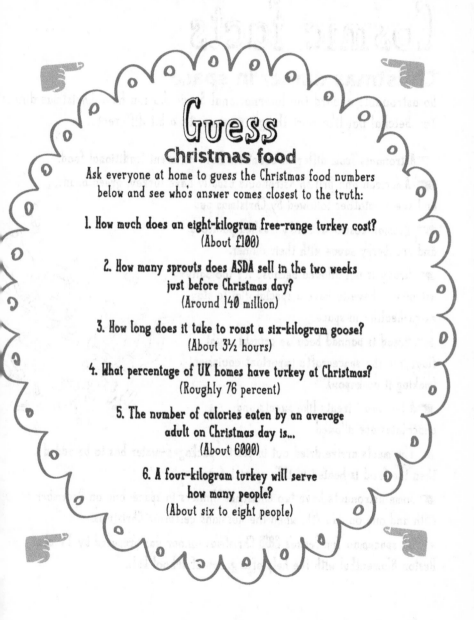

Guess
Christmas food

Ask everyone at home to guess the Christmas food numbers
below and see who's answer comes closest to the truth:

1. How much does an eight-kilogram free-range turkey cost?
(About £100)

2. How many sprouts does ASDA sell in the two weeks
just before Christmas day?
(Around 140 million)

3. How long does it take to roast a six-kilogram goose?
(About 3½ hours)

4. What percentage of UK homes have turkey at Christmas?
(Roughly 76 percent)

5. The number of calories eaten by an average
adult on Christmas day is...
(About 6000)

6. A four-kilogram turkey will serve
how many people?
(About six to eight people)

Cosmic facts

Christmas dinner in space

Do astronauts aboard the International Space Station have Christmas dinner? You betcha! But like most things in space it's a bit different...

☞ Astronauts from different countries have different traditional food.

☞ American and British astronauts usually have turkey, green beans, and sweet potatoes followed by Christmas pud.

☞ Russian cosmonauts like mashed potatoes and cranberry sauce with their dinner.

☞ Gravy is not allowed because it's too salty— astronauts have to have a special diet to stay extra-healthy in space.

☞ Bread is banned because crumbs might float into the spacecraft's important equipment (making it go kapow).

☞ A few small treats like sweets and chocolates are allowed.

☞ The meals arrive dried out in plastic packages—water has to be added then the food is heated in ISS's special oven.

☞ Some astronauts have two Christmas dinners in space: one on December 25th and one on Jan 7th, when the Russians celebrate Christmas.

☞ UK spaceman Tim Peake's 2015 Christmas dinner was prepared by TV chef Heston Blumenthal with the help of a group of school kids.

Games

Alphabet chatter

This is a good game to play around the dinner table when you've had your Christmas meal. It's best played with four or more but any number over two can play.

HOW TO PLAY:
- The youngest person goes first. He or she says something about the dinner that must begin with A (a sentence or comment, not a single word).
- The conversation continues clockwise. The second person must say something about the meal that starts with B. It should flow on from the first one.
- The next person makes a remark starting with C and so on.
- There is no winner and no one is out—it's just a fun game to enjoy.

FOR EXAMPLE:
'**A**re you ready for the next course yet?'
'**B**ut I thought we'd finished.'
'**C**ourse not—there's still the cheese and biscuits to come.'
'**D**on't you want any?'
'**E**ven I couldn't eat any more.'

Games
Table tinker

Play this game when everyone has finished eating but the table has not yet been cleared. The aim of the game is to spot small changes that other players have made to the things on the table. This game can be played with as many people as you like!

HOW TO PLAY:

- **The oldest person sitting around the table goes first.**
- All of the other players must turn their chair around and cover their eyes so they can't see what's going on.
- **The oldest person makes one small change to something on the table. For example, moving a dish to a different place, putting a spoon in another bowl or turning an empty glass upside down. The change must be large enough that the other players will notice (so you can't just move the salt by two millimeters!)**
- Once the oldest player is ready everyone turns around and tries to spot the change.
- **Take turns to call out answers by moving clockwise around the table so that everyone gets a go.**

Memory game

This is a classic memory game to play around the dinner table once it has been cleared. You will need to ask someone to prepare the game in advance. As many players as you like can join in.

HOW TO PLAY:

• **Each player needs their own piece of paper and a pen.**

• Someone brings in a tray covered in twelve small objects and places it in the middle of the table. (These can be any everyday items from around the house that everyone knows the name of.)

• **Everyone has one minute to look at the items on the tray before it is covered with a tea towel.**

• Once the tray is covered up everyone must try and write down as many objects as they can remember.

• **The person who remembers the most is the winner! But there might be more than one winner in a game like this so you'll have to share your glory!**

If you want to make the game harder just try adding more than twelve items to the tray!

Up Jenkins!

This is a noisy, fun game to play around the dinner table after you've finished your meal. It needs at least six people to play in two teams of three. You also need a coin.

HOW TO PLAY:

• **The two teams face each other across the table.**
• The team with the youngest person goes first.
• **This team takes the coin and starts passing it between them underneath the table so the other team can't see where it is and who has it. To confuse the other team the players can also pretend to pass the coin underneath the table.**
• Each player on the team without the coin has one go to say 'Up Jenkins!' When this happens, all of the players on the team that has been passing the coin underneath the table must lift up both hands as quickly as they can and then immediately slam them down on the table.
• **Whoever said 'Up Jenkins' on the opposing team then has to guess who has the coin underneath their hand. If the guesser is right, their team gets a point. However, if they are wrong then the other team gets a point.**
• The teams take turns to have the coin. The winners are the first team to score ten points.

Lists

Christmas meals around the world

Not everyone has turkey at Christmas. People around the world have a huge range of different traditional dishes. Here are a few examples of popular dishes:

Finland:

A large ham with rutabaga (swede) casserole, served on Christmas Eve.

Sweden:

A large selection of dishes including smoked salmon, ham, pickled herring, beetroot salad, cabbage, meatballs, sausage and potato salad, fish, and various cheeses.

France:

Lots of expensive foods including smoked salmon or lobster and oysters.

Czech Republic:

Fried carp with eggs and potato salad.

Jamaica:

Goat curry or oxtail with rice and peas.

New Zealand:

A traditional British-style meal, or a barbecue (Christmas is in summer).

Iceland:

Smoked lamb, ptarmigan stew (a game bird), goose, or even puffin, followed by spiced rice pudding.

Japan:

Kentucky Fried Chicken (yes, really, as a result of a VERY successful advertising campaign that started in the 1970s).

CHRISTMAS CRACKERS

Talk

Have a giggle chatting through these with someone.

- What's the best cracker gift you ever had?
- What's the worst?
- If you could have any gift small enough to fit in a cracker, what would you choose?
- Instead of a paper hat, come up with a new item to put in a cracker.

Cracking facts

- One hundred years ago, crackers were used right through the year to celebrate crazes or events like the invention of the radio.
- The world's longest Christmas cracker was made by parents at a primary school in Buckinghamshire in 2001. It was more than sixty meters long!
- The first Christmas crackers contained sweets.
- The cracker bang is made by a tiny amount of explosive chemicals rubbing together.

Guess

Can you work out the answer to these dreadful cracker jokes? Ask your friends and family and see what answers they come up with! (The answers are on page 151.)

(The answers are on page 151.)

5. What do you call a dairy farmer at the North Pole?

6. Which animals are always wet at Christmas?

1. What do monkeys sing at Christmas?

7. What did Adam say to his wife on the day before Christmas?

2. What do you get if you cross Santa with a duck?

3. Which athlete is warmest at Christmas?

4. What does Santa do when his elves are naughty?

Score

Rate these cracker jokes out of ten:

What do you get when you cross a snowman with a vampire?
Frostbite.

Why did no one bid for Rudolph and Prancer on eBay?
Because they were two deer.

What is James Bond's favorite Christmas food?
Mince spies.

What position does Father Christmas play at football?
Santa forward.

What is a dog's favorite carol?
Bark the Herald Angels Sing.

What's an ig?
An Eskimo's house without a toilet.

Jokes

Good cracker jokes

Christmas cracker jokes aren't all bad!

What do carol singers wear when they go to bed?
Silent nighties.

What is the best Christmas present in the world?
A broken drum because you can't beat it.

How does Good King Wenceslas like his pizzas?
Deep pan, crisp and even.

What did one snowman say to the other snowman?
Can you smell carrots?

What's white and goes up?
A confused snowflake.

So-bad-they're-good cracker jokes

What does Father Christmas get if he doesn't cut his fingernails?
Santa claws.

What kind of motorbike does Santa ride?
A Holly Davidson.

What carol is often heard in the desert?
O Camel Ye Faithful.

What do you drain your sprouts with at Christmas?
An advent colander.

What beats its chest and swings from Christmas cake to Christmas cake?
Tarzipan.

Get creative

Write your own Christmas cracker joke

1 Most cracker jokes are based on puns. A pun is a joke which uses a word that sounds or means the same as another. For example:

What do you sing at a snowman's birthday party?
Freeze a jolly good fellow!
(Freeze sounds like 'For he's')

2 Think of words or names connected with Christmas such as Santa, holly, present, carol, snow, robin, and so on. Now try to find another word which sounds like these Christmas words. For example:

There's a Christmas carol called
'Ding Dong Merrily on High'
Ding Dong sounds a bit like *King Kong*.

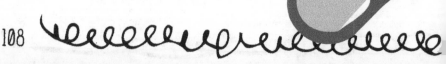

3 Now think of something that can connect your new word to Christmas in some way. King Kong is a giant gorilla, so the joke could be:

What is a gorilla's favorite Christmas carol?
King Kong Merrily on High!

4 Joke writing is hard! Keep trying and don't be put off if people groan when you tell them your joke—that's normal!

Write your best joke here:

Get Creative

Cracking crackers

Follow the instructions below and have a go at making your own Christmas crackers.

YOU WILL NEED:
- Cardboard tubes
- Cracker snaps (you can buy these from a toy shop or craft shop)
- A4 piece of paper (to wrap your cracker in)
- Ribbon or string
- Glue
- Something to put inside your cracker (such as small sweets)
- Jokes (use the jokes you came up with on page 109)

1 Divide your piece of paper into three sections.

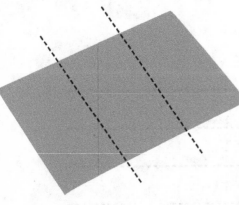

2 Next, cut up the cardboard tube into three parts and make sure that one piece is a bit bigger than the others (this will be the middle part of your cracker).

3 Stick down both ends of your cracker snap (don't stick the middle part down or it won't bang!).

4 Next place the three parts of your cardboard tube in the middle of each of the divided sections of your paper.

5 Roll the paper onto the tube, tucking in the edges neatly. Then glue down the edge of the cracker.

6 Tie the paper at one end of the middle of your cracker using some ribbon.

7 Drop any toys, sweets, chocolates, jokes, or paper hats into the untied end. Once this has been done, tie that end up with ribbon too.

Now you can decorate your cracker in whatever way you like!

CHRISTMAS FILMS AND TV

Talk

Get together with friends and family and see what everyone says.

Box of delights

What's your favorite Christmas film?
What's your favorite Christmas TV show?
Which Christmas film can't you stand?
What did you used to love watching on TV when you were little?

Film fun

Do you like these kinds of films? Give each type a rating out of ten

- Wacky
- Weepy
- Old school
- Creepy
- Funny

- Action
- Mystery
- Animated
- Musical
- True story

Challenge

Typos (typing goofs) crop up everywhere! And sometimes TV guides accidentally make mistakes with the names of movies shown over Christmas. Look at the typo-tastic list below—can you tell what the real film is? The answers are on page 151.

1. Chicken Bun
2. Coal Runnings
3. Tof Story
4. Pugs in Boots
5. How to Brain your Dragon
6. The Legs Movie
7. Danny McPhee
8. Fantastic Mr Sox
9. Despicable Ma

10. The Hound of Music
11. Gary Poppins
12. Chitty Chitty Bing Bong
13. It's a Wonderful Lift
14. Elk
15. Bog

Think of a list of your favorite movies and have a go at writing some of your own messed up listings!

----------------------------   ----------------------------

----------------------------   ----------------------------

----------------------------   ----------------------------

Choose

Christmas TV

What would you rather watch?

A sitcom or reality TV show?
A cooking program or drama?
A wildlife documentary or cartoon?
A soap or quiz show?

Christmas films

Pick which movie you'd prefer to watch over Christmas.

- Scrooge or Elf?
- Mickey's Christmas Carol or The Muppet Christmas Carol?
- The Lion, the Witch and the Wardrobe or The Polar Express?
- How the Grinch Stole Christmas or The Snowman?
- Santa Claus or The Nightmare Before Christmas?

Score

There are always hundreds of films shown at Christmas. Some
of them are crackers and some of them are turkeys! Give
these movies a rating based on the stars below.

❄	I'd rather watch my toenails grow
❄ ❄	Borrrring
❄ ❄ ❄	Not bad, passes the time
❄ ❄ ❄ ❄	Like it
❄ ❄ ❄ ❄ ❄	LOVE it!

Pirates of the Caribbean

Chicken Run

ET   Bambi   Shrek

Frozen

Indiana Jones and the Temple of Doom

Home Alone

Kung Fu Panda

Harry Potter and the Half-Blood Prince

Mini quiz

Do you watch too much TV at Christmas?

There's only one way to find out—do this quiz.

1. How many TVs are there in your house?
a) One
b) Two to three
c) Give me an hour while I count them

2. What is your pet rabbit called?
a) Peter
b) Scooby
c) Channel 5

3. If you accidentally broke your nose, where would you go?
a) The local hospital
b) Holby City
c) Doctor Who

4. Who is your greatest hero?
a) Florence Nightingale
b) David Attenborough
c) The Chuckle Brothers

5. Where will you be going on holiday next year?
a) Cornwall
b) Downton Abbey
c) Harry Hill

6. If there was a power cut what would you do?
a) Read a book by torchlight
b) Watch a DVD on a laptop
c) Waaaaaaaaaa!

What your answers mean:

Mostly 'A's:
No danger of you becoming a couch zombie—well done!

Mostly 'B's:
Amber alert: your TV watching is dangerously high.

Mostly 'C's:
Why are you reading this— you're missing the shampoo adverts.

Challenge

Can you name...

1. Four films beginning with B?
2. Three TV shows beginning with W?
3. Two films which feature elephants?
4. Three actors who have played James Bond?
5. Which classic Disney animated films feature these characters:

a) Pumbaa
b) Princess Elsa
c) Baloo
d) Jiminy Cricket
e) Belle
f) Jafar
g) Dory
h) Thumper
i) Ursula
j) Mushu

The answers are on page 152.

Get Creative

Mangled movies

Here are ten films which are just a little mixed up.
See if you can find the ten real titles.
The answers are on page 152.

1. The Lion Factory
2. Finding the Beast
3. The Iron King
4. Beauty and the Goblet of Fire
5. Honey I Shrunk the Museum
6. One Hundred and One Kids
7. High School Giant
8. Harry Potter and Nemo
9. Night at the Musical
10. Charlie and the Chocolate Dalmatians

Design a film poster for one of the
crazy mangled movies above.

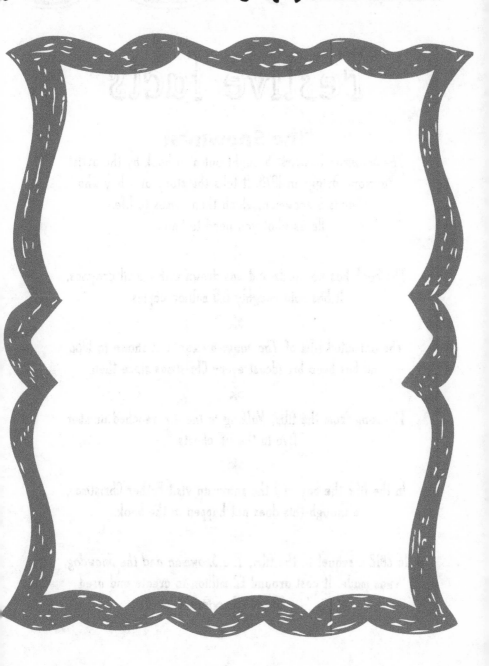

Festive facts

The Snowman

The Snowman was first brought out as a book by the artist
Raymond Briggs in 1978. It tells the story of a boy who
builds a snowman, which then comes to life.
Here's what you need to know...

The book has no words and was drawn with pencil crayons.
It has sold roughly 8.5 million copies.

The animated film of *The Snowman* was first shown in 1982
and has been broadcast every Christmas since then.

The song from the film, *Walking in the Air*, reached number
five in the UK charts.

In the film the boy and the snowman visit Father Christmas,
although this does not happen in the book.

In 2012 a sequel to the film, *The Snowman and the Snowdog*,
was made. It cost around £2 million to create and used
200,000 drawings!

Jokes
Guess the film!

Try these out on your friends and family:

Which film is about Scrooge in the desert?
A Christmas Camel.

Which film is about a cricket referee in outer space?
The Umpire Strikes Back.

Which film is about a king who is good at going up ladders and fighting evil?
The Lord of the Rungs.

Which film is about a butcher who is trapped in a world of scary dinosaurs?
Jurassic Pork.

Which film is about a boy wizard who likes home baking?
Harry Potter and the Philosopher's Scone.

Which film is about a very small man who foils some burglars at his house?
Gnome Alone.

Which film is about telling the time in Narnia?
The Lion, the Watch and the Wardrobe.

Which film is about a smelly bear who does martial arts?
Kung Phew Panda.

Which World War II film is about a man getting out of a wooden box?
The Crate Escape.

Which film is about a jungle animal who never tells the truth?
The Lying King.

THE CHRISTMAS STORY

Talk

Stars, angels, and mangers

What is your favorite part of the Christmas story?

If you were a film director, which two of these scenes would you most like to film?

★ **The angel appearing to Mary**

★ The wise men following the star

★ **King Herod plotting to find the child**

★ Mary and Joseph travelling to Bethlehem

★ **The innkeeper turning them away**

★ The shepherds visiting the new baby

★ **The wise men presenting their gifts**

Nativity plays

Were you ever in a nativity play? Which part did you have?
What is your best memory of nativity plays and why?
Which part did you always want?
What do you like or dislike about nativity plays?

Jokes

Nativity pun fun

Do you know any groaners
like these?

**What's Gabriel's favorite
pudding?**
Angel Delight

**Why did Joseph go to
Bethlehem even though he
didn't want to?**
He came to his census

**Why was the hotel in Bethlehem
dusty?**
They had no broom at the inn

Why were Mary and Joseph happy?
They had a stable relationship

**How did Mary and Joseph know
that Jesus was 4 kilograms when
he was born?**
They had a weigh in a manger

**Why weren't there any children at
the stable in Bethlehem?**
Because of manger danger

Fun lists

Infant nativity play checklist

Infant school nativity plays are always sweet and fun to watch and they often feature mishaps, gaffes, and other funny happenings. How many of these have you seen?

MARY
Forgets her lines
Drops the baby Jesus

JOSEPH
Wipes his runny nose on his costume
Can't say 'Nazareth'

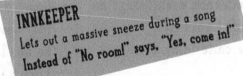

INNKEEPER
Lets out a massive sneeze during a song
Instead of "No room!" says, "Yes, come in!"

ANGELS
Pick their noses
Clearly need the loo

SHEPHERDS
Accidentally poke the donkey with their crooks
Wave and say, "Hiya mum!"

KINGS/WISE MEN
Drop the gifts
Say 'Frankenstein' instead of frankincense

DONKEY
Trips over the manger
Starts to cry

Challenges

Christmas story puzzles

Can you work out who these people from the Christmas story are? The letters of their names are a tiny bit mixed up...
Answers on page 152.

POJESH   **SAW MINE**   YARM

OK HERDING   RED PHESH

Can you unjumble this list of things that are usually mentioned in the Christmas story?
Answers on page 152.

RATS   NIN   ME GRAN

GLOD   YOKEND

BE LAST

NIC FERN SNAKE

Make your own

Now have a go at jumbling up the following and see if your friends and family can figure out what they are:

BETHLEHEM

DESERT   NAZARETH

Words in words

How many words can you make out of the letters of BETHLEHEM?

Here's what to aim for:
8—Good
10—Impressive
12—Wow!
15—Sensational!
(Answers on page 153.)

Fascinating Facts

How some Christmas traditions began

Christmas Eve

Many churches have special services at midnight on Christmas Eve. This is because some people believe that Jesus was born at midnight.

December 25th

No one knows the real date that Jesus was born and so for a long time Christmas Day was celebrated on different dates. The first people to celebrate on December 25th were the Romans about 1,700 years ago, when the Emperor decided to follow Christianity.

The Star of Bethlehem

Some people believe that the star followed by the wise men may have really been a comet. Others think that the star may have been bright planets lining up in the night sky to make an extra-bright object. Today a star decoration is often put on top of a Christmas tree.

The Twelve Days of Christmas

The twelve days start on December 25th, when Jesus was said to have been born, and finish on January 5th, the day before the wise men traditionally visited Mary and Joseph with gifts.

Get Creative

WHAT YOU NEED:
- A piece of A4 coloured paper (wrapping paper which is shiny on one side is best)
- Scissors
- Glue

Make a 3D paper star

Create your own star decoration by following the directions below:

WHAT TO DO:

1 Fold the piece of A4 paper in half longways:

2 Next, cut along the fold with a scissors so that you end up with two long strips.

3 Fold over the end of one strip (the fold should be about two centimeters wide).

4 Turn the strip over and fold the same end two centimeters over itself again. Turn over and repeat. Keep doing this until the whole piece is folded in a 'concertina' fashion:

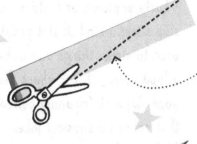

5 Draw a diagonal dotted line (starting about a third of the way along one edge) across the folded page and carefully cut the folded shape along the dotted line:

6 Open the piece of paper out, keeping the non-pointed ends together. You'll see half a star shape appear.

7 Repeat all this with the other strips of paper then glue the two halves together to make a star.

PANTOMIME TIME

Fascinating Facts

Panto history

Pantomimes are plays that are usually performed at Christmas. They're musical, they're funny, they have loads of silly costumes. Here's a little bit about how panto began...

• Pantomimes have their roots in ancient Greece, although some people at the time thought they were too rude!

• Lots of panto characters come from a type of Italian street theatre called *commedia dell'arte* that dates from the sixteenth century.

• The first pantomimes in British theatres had no talking or singing—only dancing and mime!

• Early pantomimes featured a slap stick: a kind of flat paddle used to strike things and make a loud noise. This is where the word slapstick (meaning comedy that relies on physical jokes such as falling over, bumping into things, etc.) comes from.

• Eventually, pantomimes became based on fairy stories and nursery rhymes, using music, dance, slapstick comedy, jokes, special effects, and encouraging the audience to join in.

• Today, most pantomimes in UK theatres feature famous people in the main roles, for example the Dame, a comic character who is usually the hero's mother.

Jokes
Cinderella funnies

One of the most popular pantomimes is Cinderella—you might know some of these Cinderella jokes but you won't know them all!

What's big, grey, and wears glass slippers?
Cinderellaphant.

What's hairy and helps Cinderella?
The furry godmother.

Who bought Cinderella fish and chips?
Her fairy codmother.

Who bought Cinderella chocolate drops?
Buttons.

What did Cinderella say while she was waiting for her photos?
Some day my prints will come.

Why was Cinderella no good at cricket?
She kept running away from the ball.

Why was Cinderella no good at football?
Her coach was a pumpkin.

Challenge

Staging Jack and the Beanstalk

Jack and the Beanstalk is another of the most popular Christmas pantomimes performed each year. It tells the tale of poor Jack who is tricked into selling his mother's precious cow, Daisy, in return for some magic beans. The beans grow into a huge beanstalk, which Jack climbs and finds a giant's castle at the top of it. Jack grabs some golden treasures (including a hen that lays golden eggs) from the giant and then quickly climbs down the beanstalk, chopping it down, and finishing off the giant who falls to his death.

Imagine you were in charge of producing this pantomime. Can you think of ways to solve these problems on stage:

1. How to create Daisy the cow.

2. How to make a giant beanstalk grow.

3. How to represent the inside of the giant's castle.

4. How to show the giant.

5. How to make a hen that lays golden eggs.

6. How Jack can chop down the beanstalk (which is needed for the next show, remember!).

Amazing facts

Did you know?

Pantomimes don't often follow the same rules as other stage plays!

- ✪ The leading young male character in a pantomime is traditionally played by a woman.
- ⊙ The leading older female character (the Dame) is usually played by a man.
- ✪ Most pantomimes have an animal—most often a comic horse played by two actors in costume.
- ⊙ The good fairy and the hero always enter from the right side of the stage.
- ✪ The villain or baddie always enters from the left side of the stage.

Get creative

Be a costume designer

THE GENIE FROM ALADDIN

Pantomime costumes are always spectacular and special. They feature big, bold designs with vibrant colors and lots of sparkle. Now is your chance to get creative and design a pantomime costume. Choose one of the characters listed below, or pick your own!

THE BALL GOWN FOR CINDERELLA

Lists
Bad Pantos
Something has gone shockingly
wrong with these pantomime names!
Can you add your own silly versions?

Beauty and the Beast	Beauty and the Beef	
Jack and the Beanstalk	Jock and the Mean Stork	
The Snow Queen	The Slow Queen	
Puss in Boots	Fuss in Boots	
Cinderella	Chinderella	
The Wizard of Oz	The Wozard of Iz	
Aladdin	Aliddon	
Dick Whittington and his Cat	Duck Whittington and his Hat	
Peter Pan	Peter Pants	
Sleeping Beauty	Sweeping Booty	
Robin Hood	Sobin Hood	
Mother Goose	Brother Goose	
Babes in the Wood	Bakes in the Wood	
Snow White and the Seven Dwarves	Snob White and the Seven Dweebs	

CHRISTMAS AROUND THE WORLD

Talk

Get together with friends and family and answer the questions below.

Home or away?
• What's the best thing about Christmas at home?
• Would you like to travel somewhere for Christmas?
• If you could choose, where would you go?

Best and worst
• What are the best things about Christmas in your country?
• What are the worst things about Christmas there?

Choose

Christmas with a difference
Where would you rather spend Christmas?

✳ In the Bahamas or in Hollywood?

✳ At the North Pole or at an oasis?

✳ On a beach or in the jungle?

✳ Up a mountain or in a cave?

✳ At sea or up in space?

✳ At Buckingham Palace (the Queen's home) or Beckingham Palace (David Beckham's home)?

✳ In a submarine or in a helicopter?

✳ With aliens or with ghosts?

Amazing facts

Curious Christmas customs around the world

Discover some fascinating facts about how different countries celebrate this festive day.

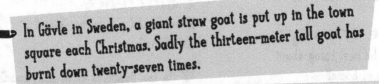

In Gävle in Sweden, a giant straw goat is put up in the town square each Christmas. Sadly the thirteen-meter tall goat has burnt down twenty-seven times.

In India, traditional Christmas trees are very hard to find so people often decorate a banana tree instead.

In Russia, people who belong to the Orthodox Church celebrate Christmas on January 7th. This is because the Orthodox Church uses a different calendar to the one used in most parts of the world.

In London every Christmas morning there is an outdoor swimming race across The Serpentine, a lake in Hyde Park. The winner of this dangerous event is awarded the Peter Pan Cup.

In Venezuela, South America, it has recently become a tradition to travel to Christmas Day church services on roller skates.

In Estonia and Finland, many families have a sauna on Christmas Eve.

In Costa Rica, it is traditional to eat the special Christmas meal after midnight on Christmas Eve.

In Greenland, a special Christmas food is raw whale skin complete with blubber (fat).

In Slovakia at Christmas some families eat a special bread and honey pudding called bobalki. It is an old custom that the head of the household flicks a spoonful of this at the ceiling to see how much sticks. (Warning: it is NOT advisable to try this at home...!).

In Ukraine, Christmas trees are not only decorated with tinsel and baubles; some people also use artificial spiders' webs complete with plastic spiders.

In some parts of Spain, model nativity scenes include small carved figures called caganers.

Guess
Nearest wins

Get your friends or family to guess the answer to the questions below.
Whoever guesses the answer closest to the truth is the winner!

How many people celebrate Christmas in Nigeria?
About eighty-five million

What is the most popular Christmas gift given in South Korea?
Money

There are no trees in Greenland so Christmas trees are often
imported from Denmark. How many miles is Denmark from
Greenland?
Over 1800 miles

What animal do people in Norway traditionally sing about at
Christmas?
A mouse

Many families in Italy have a Christmas crib. What date is this put
out?
December 8th

Jokes
Round-the-world-riddles

Which US state does
Joseph love best?
Maryland

Which country has
the most skates?
Iceland

Where's the best place to see
Father Christmas at sea?
Santa Cruz

What's the best country
for Christmas dinner?
Turkey

In which country is it
most likely to snow?
Chile

If they speak Spanish in Spain
and Swedish in Sweden, what
do they speak in Hungary?
Peckish

Where do bank managers
go for Christmas?
The Cheque Republic

Which small royals
visit Scotland each
Christmas?
The Wee Three Kings

Score

Christmas in summer

In Australia and New Zealand, December 25th is in the middle of summer! Give each of these a score out of 10 for how much you'd like them:

Eating roast turkey with salad.

Celebrating Christmas on a scorching hot day.

Never having snow at Christmas.

Having a Christmas picnic on the beach.

Swimming outdoors on New Year's Day.

Where to travel for Christmas

Have you ever wanted to fly away somewhere else for Christmas day? Rank the following countries from 1 to 10—starting with the place you'd most like to v

Canada   Fiji   Greece   New Zealand   Hong Kong

Kenya   Peru   Sweden   Thailand   UK

Challenges

Hidden countries

Christmas is celebrated all around the world. Can you work out what the jumbled up countries below are? Answers on page 153.

	4 letters	6 letters	more...
1	REPU	REFCAN	KANASPIT
2	GOTO	OLDPAN	LEGANES
3	RAIN	ECOMIX	EARIING
4	JIFI	RESAIL	THANDIAL
5	CHAIN	ANDACA	CANDILE
6	DACH	DONJAR	TEARANING

Have a go at making your own country anagrams for someone else to guess. Try these countries: Mali, Iraq, Chile, Brazil, Spain, Greece, Norway, Turkey, Mongolia, Afghanistan.

Name it

Can you name these? Answers on page 153.

1. Three countries beginning with M.
2. Four countries with two words in their name.
3. Five countries beginning with S.
4. Christmas is sometimes shortened to Xmas: what are the only two countries containing the letter 'x'?

Quiz
Christmas in Germany

True or false? How many of the statements about Christmas in Germany can you get right? Answers on page 153.

1. In Germany, Christmas trees are usually put up on December 25th.

3. Germans give each other presents on Christmas Eve.

2. Most children in Germany are given special Christmas biscuits.

4. German families usually sing carols outside on Christmas Day.

5. A traditional Christmas gift is a wooden apple.

Games
Global goodies

You'll need three or more people to play this game. Each person needs to think up a Christmas item (or present) that they've bought in a foreign country. But the item and the country must begin with the same letter! Each person must begin by saying, "I bought..."

FOR EXAMPLE:
Player 1: I bought holly in Holland
Player 2: I bought crackers in Croatia
Player 3: I bought reindeer in Romania

The first person to get stuck is out!

If you want to make the game harder then each player must repeat all of the items bought so far before adding their own to the list! For example:
"I bought holly in Holland, crackers in Croatia, reindeer in Romania, and a fairy in France."

Fangman

This is a version of the old game hangman, and you can give it a festive twist by choosing a Christmas theme. One player thinks of a place connected with Christmas and everyone else has to try and guess it!

HOW TO PLAY:

• Draw spaces for each letter of the word. For example, NORTH POLE would be set out like this: _ _ _ _ _ / _ _ _ _

• The other players must guess letters one at a time.

• The player who has thought of the Christmassy place fills in any correct letters that are guessed.

• The player who has thought of the Christmassy place fills in any correct letters that are guessed.

• But if anyone guesses a wrong letter then the first player adds a feature to the fangman drawing:

• Draw the picture in this order: head, eye, eye, nose, mouth, eyebrow, eyebrow, ear, ear, hair, fang, fang.

• Whoever guesses what the word is goes next. If no one guesses it before the whole fangman is finished, the person drawing wins.

Get creative
Your exotic Christmas

Imagine if you could have Christmas anywhere in the world! Answer each of the questions below on where you would like to go. Once you're finished draw a picture of all the answers you have given in one big scene!

What kind of Christmas tree would you have?

Where would you go?

Who would be there?

What would you have for Christmas dinner?

What might you do that is special?

What presents would you give?

One final Christmas joke...

Knock Knock,
Who's there?
Hannah
Hannah who?
Hannah partridge in a pear tree!

147

ANSWERS

Christmas Music

Merged melodies
(page 24)

The six carols are:

God Rest ye Merry Gentlemen

I Saw Three Ships

O Come All Ye Faithful

Deck the Halls

O Little Town of Bethlehem

Joy to the World

Christmas conundrum (page 24)

1. Silent Night
2. We Three Kings
3. The First Noel

Christmas Cards

Mixed up in the post
(page 36)

The mixed-up items are:

envelope

postman

greeting

Christmas card

Christmas stamp

Trees and Decorations

Jumbled up decorations (page 51)

1. star
2. holly
3. tinsel
4. fairy
5. wreath
6. bauble
7. stocking
8. candle
9. garland
10. ribbons

Christmas tree quiz
(page 60)

1. False: the first Christmas trees were put up in Germany.
2. False: it takes about ten years to grow a two-meter fir tree.
3. True.
4. True: but the candles caused lots of fires!
5. True: it is decorated with 60,000 lights!
6. False: a one-meter-tall spruce tree has about 130,000 needles.

That Man Santa
Rev Spooner's list for Santa (page 67)

1. toy car
2. football boots
3. teddy bear
4. loom bands
5. toy robot
6. guinea pig
7. snooker cue
8. dumper truck
9. jigsaw puzzle
10. robot dog
11. mobile phone
12. painting set

Reindeer quiz
(page 69)

1. Two reindeer
2. Caribou
3. True
4. Three
5. True (although not all reindeer knees click)
6. Herds
7. False: a day-old baby reindeer can run faster than an Olympic sprinter
8. Crocodiles
9. Rudolph
10. Blitzen (which means 'lightning')

The North Pole (page 73)

1. 2.5m
2. 4261m
3. 1926
4. -40 °C
5. 8: Norway, Sweden, Finland, Russia, USA (Alaska), Canada, Denmark (Greenland), Iceland

Challenge (page 73)

Here are some of the words you can make from the letters of SLEIGH BELLS:

bee, beg, big, gee, gel, his, ill, leg, lie, lee, see, she

bees, begs, bell, eels, else, glee, gels, gill, glib, heel, hell, hiss, isle, legs, less sees, sell, sigh, sill

belle, bells, beige, bilge, bless, hills, sells, shell, siege, sills

shells, sleigh

bellies, legible, legless, shells, sleighs

Yippee: Presents!

Present-giving around the world

(page 88)

1. D   5. E
2. G   6. C
3. A   7. F
4. B

Can you name? (page 90)

1. Some possible answers include: magic set, magnets, magnifying glass, Mario Kart®, marshmallows, Meccano®, metal detector, Mickey Mouse® puppet, microscope, mirror, mobile, models, money, Monopoly®, mountain bike, Mr Bean® DVD, mug.

2. Some possible answers are: jars, bottles, spectacles, glasses for drinks, vases, bowls, mirrors, paperweights.

3. Some possible answers are: B&Q®, Barratts®, Boots®, Body Shop®, Blackwells®, Burton Menswear, Budgens®.

4. Some possible answers are: cactus, cake stand, calendar, calculator, camera,

camping gear, can opener, candles, canoe, cap, car stickers, cards, cardigan, casserole dish, cat basket, CD holder, chain, cheese, cherries, chess set, chocolates, clock, clogs, clothes, coat, coffee, computer, cookbook, corkscrew, cosmetics, crossword book, crystal, cufflinks, cups, cushion.

Odd one out (page 90)
In the bath.

Yum Yum, Christmas Dinner

Guess
(page 105)
1. Jungle Bells
2. Christmas quackers
3. A long jumper
4. He gives them the sack
5. An Eskimoo
6. Reindeer
7. It's Christmas Eve!

Christmas Films and TV

Challenge (page 113)
1. Chicken Run
2. Cool Runnings
3. Toy Story
4. Puss in Boots
5. How to Train your Dragon
6. The Lego Movie
7. Nanny McPhee
8. Fantastic Mr Fox
9. Despicable Me
10. The Sound of Music
11. Mary Poppins
12. Chitty Chitty Bang Bang
13. It's a Wonderful Life
14. Elf
15. Big

Can you name... (page 117)

Possible answers include: Babe, Back to the Future (1-3), Bambi, Batman (various), Beauty and the Beast, Beethoven, Big, Black Beauty.

2. Possible answers include: The Weakest Link, What's New Scooby Doo?, Who Wants to be a Millionaire?, Winner Takes All, Walk on the Wild Side, Wild, The Wombles.

3. Possible answers include: Dumbo, The Jungle Book, Indiana Jones and the Temple of Doom, Horton Hears a Who, Tarzan.

4. The actors who have played James Bond on film are Pierce Brosnan, Sean Connery, Daniel Craig, Timothy Dalton, George Lazenby, and Roger Moore.

5. Classic Disney animated films:
a) The Lion King
b) Frozen
c) The Jungle Book
d) Pinocchio
e) Beauty and the Beast
f) Aladdin
g) Finding Nemo
h) Bambi
i) The Little Mermaid
j) Mulan

Mangled movies (page 118)

1. The Lion King
2. Finding Nemo
3. The Iron Giant
4. Beauty and the Beast
5. Honey I Shrunk the Kids
6. One Hundred and One Dalmatians
7. High School Musical
8. Harry Potter and The Goblet of Fire
9. Night at the Museum
10. Charlie and the Chocolate Factory

The Christmas Story

Christmas story puzzles (page 126)

PEOPLE	THINGS
1. Joseph	6. star
2. wise man	7. inn
3. Mary	8. manger
4. shepherd	9. stable
5. King Herod	10. gold
	11. donkey
	12. frankincense

Words in words (page 126)

Words made from the letters of Bethlehem
Here are some of the words you can make:
be, eh, he, me
bee, bet, eel, elm, hem, lee, let, met, tee, the
beet, belt, heel, helm, meet, melt, teem, thee, them
theme
beetle, helmet

Christmas Around the World

Hidden countries

(page 143)

	3 letters	4 letters	more...
1	PERU	FRANCE	PAKISTAN
2	TOGO	POLAND	SENEGAL
3	IRAN	MEXICO	NIGERIA
4	FIJI	ISRAEL	THAILAND
5	CHINA	CANADA	ICELAND
6	CHAD	JORDAN	ARGENTINA

Name it (page 143)

1. Answers include: Macedonia, Madagascar, Malawi, Malaysia, Maldives, Mali, Malta, the Marshall Islands, Martinique, Mauritania, Mauritius, Mexico, the Federated States of Micronesia, Moldova, Monaco, Mongolia, Morocco, and Mozambique.

2. Well known examples are: Costa Rica, Czech Republic, El Salvador, North Korea, South Korea, South Africa, New Zealand, Saudi Arabia, Sri Lanka and United Kingdom (there are also others such as Burkina Faso, Cape Verde, Dominican Republic, Equatorial Guinea, San Marino, and Sierra Leone).

3. Well known examples are: Saudi Arabia, Singapore, Slovakia, South Africa, South Korea, Spain, Sri Lanka, Sudan, Sweden, Switzerland and Syria. You could also have: Saint Kitts & Nevis, Saint Lucia, Samoa, San Marino, São Tomé & Príncipe, Serbia, Seychelles, Sierra Leone, Slovenia, Solomon Islands, Somalia, South Sudan, Swaziland.

4. Luxembourg and Mexico.

Christmas in Germany (page 144)

1. false (trees are put up on 24th)
2. true
3. true
4. true
5. false
6. false

SCRIBBLE SPACE

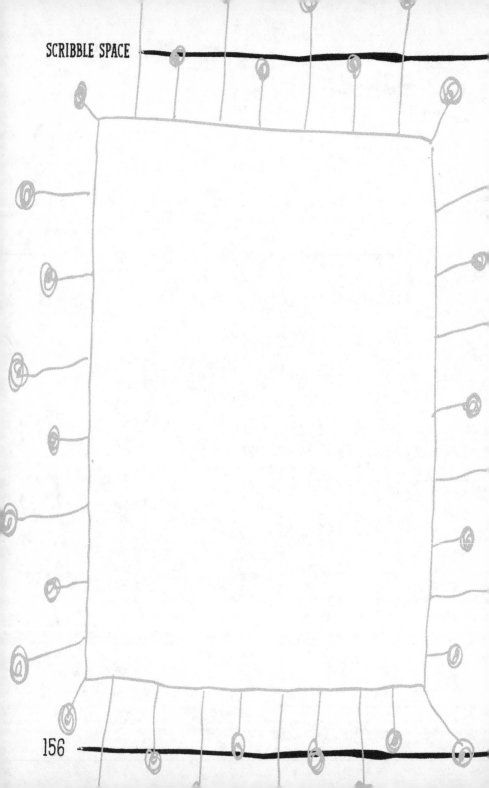

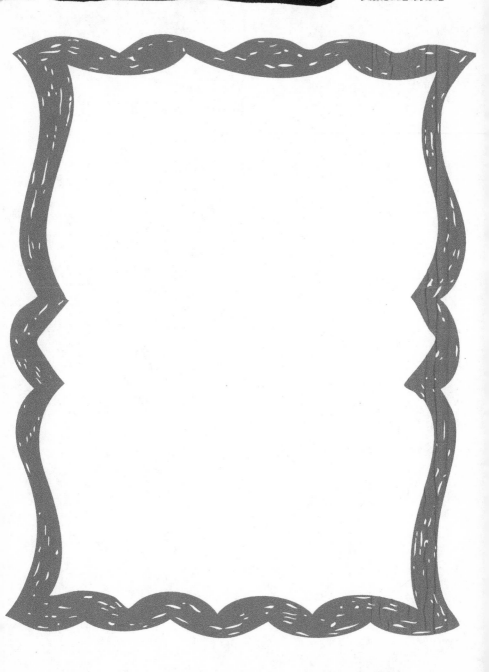

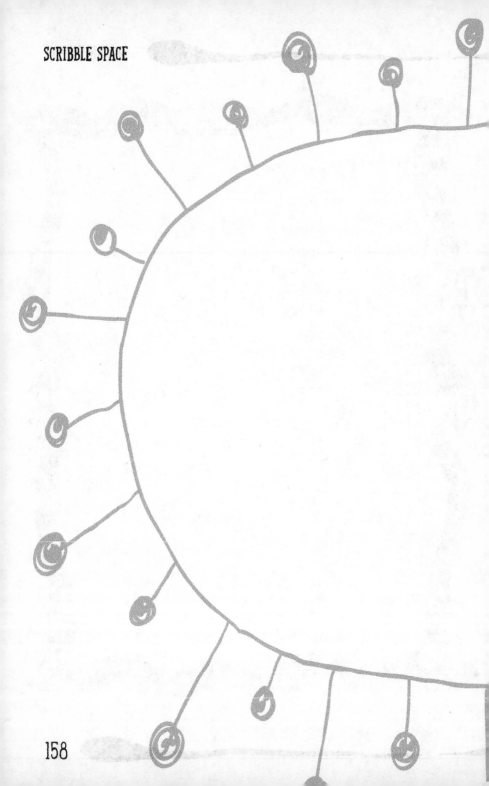

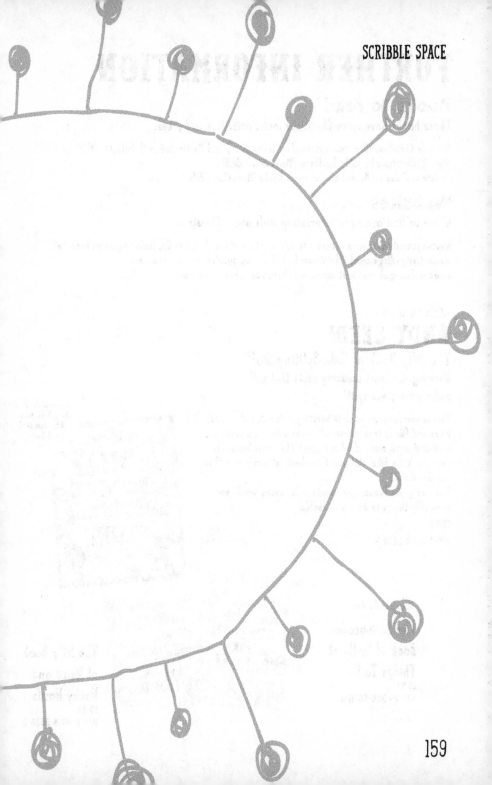

SCRIBBLE SPACE

159

FURTHER INFORMATION

Books to read

These books have more Christmas facts, activities and jokes:

Horrible Christmas (Horrible Histories) by Terry Deary and Martin Brown (Scholastic 2011)
Draw It: Christmas by Sally Kindberg (Bloomsbury 2013)
Christmas Jokes by Macmillan Children's Books (Macmillan 2013)

Websites

Where to find out more interesting stuff about Christmas:

www.whychristmas.com—a superb site full of info and fun things to do, including Xmas karaoke!
www.activityvillage.co.uk/christmas—lots of crafts, puzzles, quizzes and more.
www.carols.org.uk—not just carols but Christmas songs, facts, poems and videos.

Also Available by
ANDY SEED!
The Silly Book of Side-Splitting Stuff
Warning: Contains amazing facts that will make your sides split!

This laugh-out-loud book is bursting with silly lists, facts, jokes and funny true stories all about animals, inventions, food and much more. Find out about The Great Stink, the man who ate a bike, the world's richest cat and a sofa that can do 101mph.
Discover gross foods, epic sports fails, wacky words and even silly things to do... Unmissable!
£5.99

978-1-4088-5079-4

Winner of the Blue Peter Book Award 2015 - Best Book with Facts.

Also available:

The Antiboredom Book of Brilliant Things To Do
£5.99
978-1-4088-5076-3

The Silly Book of Weird and Wacky Words
£5.99
978-1-4088-5338-2